Marilee -
a story for those
who love these marvelous creatures.
Enjoy !
Leah July 10, 2012

Big Blue Buzzard

A Story of Love and Discovery

McLean Goodpasture Carroll

Big Blue Buzzard

A Story of Love and Discovery

Cover artwork by Brendan Donckers

Acknowledgements

There are several people I wish to thank for encouraging me to put this story to paper. The many narrations of the tale garnered countless reactions and opinions—the veracity and improbability of such an account for the most part—but almost everyone told me that I needed to write it down.

My cousin, Maxie Slack Brien, was probably the initial and most vociferous persuader, and she introduced the story to many other readers as well. My good friends, Kathryn and Rob Thompson, were the first people to offer editing ideas, both spending quite a bit of time and effort on the first draft, and to them I am ever grateful. Alice Prince, a friend from my affiliation with the Lake Washington Saddle Club, gave me invaluable pointers on sentence structure that were brand new to me. My childhood buddy, Molly Walling, who holds an MFA in writing and teaches the subject at the University of North Carolina in Asheville, was a terrific inspiration. She spent a lot of time reading, offering insights and insisting that I had potential as a story teller. "Keep plugging away at it, good buddy." Thank you Molly.

Many friends, more than I can truthfully count, have expressed encouragement, but I must give recognition to Julie Hull, a riding pal, who, after completing a course in editing, spent countless hours pouring over the manuscript for punctuation and grammar issues. Her eye is keen and her suggestions were well received.

If it weren't for Bonnie Ward and her mother, Maurine Wilcoxon, as well as Maurine's Personal Assistant, Andrea Evans, for introducing me to CreateSpace and the exciting opportunity for self-publishing, the realization of this book would have remained a dream. Their help was invaluable.

Lastly I wish to thank my husband and children for believing my story, whether it is an act or real, and to my extended family as well for making me who I am.

I dedicate this book to the Spirit of Buzz for teaching me that life on earth, and perhaps beyond, is much more fun if you open your heart and mind. And I give thanks for the continuing quest for understanding.

I also wish to thank my husband, Bill, for the loving generosity that allowed my discovery to even occur.

Big Blue Buzzard

A Story of Love and Discovery

Part I

Childhood

I would travel only by horse, if I had a choice.

Linda McCartney

When riding a horse we leave our fear, troubles and sadness behind on the ground.

Juli Carson, historian

Chapter 1

"Hey *Jimmy*," I hollered from the dimly lit hayloft of the barn. "Do you know if this is straw or hay up here?" I needed straw for bedding a horse's stall and couldn't see which was which.

"Int's oants uhney, buhnt they'll eant int ihnyway."

"Jimmy, you weird-o," I said cracking up, "you're a nut case! "

"What did he just say they will eat?" asked my buddy, Robin, giggling.

"He said this stuff is oats! *He knows we know the oats are in the feed room.*" I bellowed to be sure he heard me.

Chuckling rose from the aisle of the barn below. Jimmy was the farrier for the horses at the Sullins College barn. Not many could understand his cleft palate-impaired speech, but I could, and I adored him. Always happy, with many a trick up his sleeve, Jimmy

1

never failed to amuse me. There was no way he could know what lay in the loft of that barn, but it didn't stop him from trying to hoodwink me. He was among the many humorous and nurturing threads woven into the tapestry of my youth. It was a childhood that early on led to a love of horses.

I cannot recall a time when I did not worship the *equus caballus*. A dim memory lingers of my mother allowing a man to hoist me onto the bare back of a large farm horse to trot around his driveway. Probably no more than five years old, I'm sure the man must have held me on. But the smell and texture of that ample mane in my face and hands and the exhilarating feeling of power stayed with me. Surely my mother tired of my pleading and whining after that day because all I *ever* wanted to do was ride.

Luckily, our home was near a big bustling riding barn in Bristol, Virginia. Sullins College, a women's junior college, had a riding program open to the public, and it was there that I took English hunt-seat riding lessons for eleven years. The college campus, situated high on a hill looking southward over a wide expanse of Bristol neighborhoods, was a beautiful example of red brick Georgian architecture. Even at an early age I felt a sense of pride in living near such a beautiful place.

The barn was situated in the rear of the campus, halfway down the back of that high wooded hill. One found their way there by either a steep dirt path down through the trees or by way of a beautiful tree-lined gravel drive that passed a faculty home, a large outdoor arena and the small humble abode of the barn groomsman. The arena, sitting at the lowest point of the property, adjoined a field with a jump course that featured seven varied permanent obstacles and a large knoll that rose rather steeply to the north.

The barn was a big barn. Long and white, it housed perhaps twenty horses, a small indoor ring, a large tack room and an office. Like most barns the stalls were situated along the sides with a large aisle in the middle; but unlike most barns, the interior wood was whitewashed, reflecting lots of light and giving the area a bright cheery air. Every spare moment I had was spent at that barn. If I couldn't ride, I would groom and help feed or just plain sit and watch. I drove the beleaguered groomsman insane, I am sure, for I was there almost every day after school and all day on Saturday.

Barbara Hatcher, my riding instructor who was surely equally harassed, practically raised me. She humored my desire for horses from age seven to eighteen (along with countless other girls in Bristol) and allowed me the opportunity to experience an unfettered joy of loving those magnificent creatures.

Eleven years is a long period to relate to one person, for certain, but what is even more certain is that her teaching went far beyond my learning to ride. She taught me love and responsibility in caring for animals. She taught me to be tough, gentle and humble and to have grace in winning and in losing. If, indeed, it takes a village to raise a child then Barbara's corner of my small world was the most visited.

The horses at Sullins were a diverse bunch, and I fell in love with nearly all of them at one time or another during my youth. Lawman, a roan quarter horse with a perfect white circle on his forehead was so special that he was my first *boyfriend*. When riding him if you pressed a certain spot on his back, right behind the saddle, he would give a little buck. He bucked harder if you pressed harder—a clever little trick. Field Mouse or "Mousie", a dark bay, was another favorite. He was distinctive in that he had lop-ears that looked like airplane wings. An enormous buckskin named Gunsmoke had a perfect diamond marking smack dab in the middle of his big nose. Sam was a white and tan piebald with a curious characteristic when wet—his skin turned pink and dark blue!

It is said that when you can recite the names of every horse at the riding school where you ride in alphabetical order—backwards and forwards—then you know you are truly horse-mad. Let me see…Chesterfield, Chief, China Boy, Goldbrick, Gunsmoke, Lawman, Martini, Mousie, Notorious, Sam, Shadow…!

All of these wonderful animals (and there were many more) were my special childhood friends, but still, I *yearned* for a horse of my very own. My grandfather always joked that he was going to buy one for me, a steed with three gaits—start, stumble and fall down—and I always laughed at that joke. I would punch him and tell him how mean he was, but I would laugh. The dream, though, of having a mount that was *mine* never dimmed. I had friends, who owned horses, and they were always generous with their invitations to ride, but it still was never quite the same as having one that belonged to only me.

One such generous friend was my buddy Robin Arnold, and a favorite memory is one of riding with Robin at her family farm in Rural Retreat, Virginia. I loved going with her to her family's properties because they always had several varieties of four-legged beasts—horses, mules, burrows, cows and dogs—and her father always indulged our constant requests to ride. We rode just about anything that would allow us to jump on its back, and our courage was boundless.

We were probably eleven or twelve years old in this particular memory: We donned our *bathing suits* and hopped on a couple of horses to gallop the open pastures. After racing around, whooping and hollering (narrowly missing a virtually invisible wire fence and surely a resultant injury), we headed back to the barn. My horse, apparently fed up with our silly antics, decided to buck me off into a stream adjacent to the farmhouse. I sailed grandly right over his head onto the rockiest creek bed you can imagine, and landing on those stones hurt like the dickens. But I had to laugh. I was suitably dressed for the occasion.

Look Ma—no hands! I guess I loved horses at a very
young age. The picture of my brother taken the same
day reveals otherwise. He was crying his eyes out! I
wish I had it to share.

Ready for the Sullins College horseshow
when I was 12 years old.

Riding Shadow at the show.

Mousie at the Kingsport horseshow. Those ears never moved!

Line-up at Kingsport horseshow. Next to me is my buddy Robin Arnold on Notorious. Gunsmoke, with the diamond nose, is far right.

Two attempts at a portrait with Lawman, my
favorite horse. I like the first one better—he's
being a clown.

Chapter 2

As the years passed with more and more time in the saddle, I got better at staying *in* the saddle, and there was nothing I enjoyed more. I was sixteen when an incredible opportunity arose to ride and train a Quarter Horse that belonged to Rip Repass, a doctor in town. He invited me into his barn Four Winds, a Western Quarter Horse establishment, to show me a brand-new English jumping saddle and bridle. I complimented him on their fine quality, wondering why in the world he was showing them to me. He then pointed out the window to a pasture full of new horses he had just purchased and said, "Get out there and pick a horse, Lean. It is time I had a jumper in this barn, and I want you to train it."

I was dumbfounded. Why would Dr. Repass ask *me* to train a horse when he could employ any number of professionals? I couldn't believe what I had just heard.

"I'm not sure I understand, Dr. Repass. I...I...I'm confused."

"Well, it's not for you to worry about or understand. I just need you to help me teach one of those horses to jump. Now take this halter and go see which one you like."

It was a command I immediately and joyously obeyed. There were at least twenty horses in that pasture. Imagine walking in with a halter and lead rope and trying to pick out just one. They were all so different and handsome, and I had absolutely no idea what I was looking for or even *doing* in that pasture. How in creation was I going to choose? What expertise could I possibly have in determining a suitable animal?

Well, it turned out the horse picked me. He was not very big—probably fifteen hands two or three inches—and was dun-colored with a dark stripe down his back, much like a Rhodesian ridgeback hound. His mane had been roached, or shaved off, but it was growing out, making him look like a punk kid sporting a Mohawk hairdo. His left buttock had a nasty-looking scar that was the result of a run-in with barbed wire, but he otherwise looked clean. He was *not* the most perfect example of a fine English hunter—he was a little cow pony—but when curiosity got the better of him and he left the herd to check me out, I knew I was toast.

I named that horse Country Squire, and the experiences I had that year were extraordinary. My good friend, Meredith Mitchell, kept her horse nearby, and we spent hours and hours exploring places unseen and schooling our horses over jumps that her father had built. The complete freedom we were given during that time in our adolescence was astonishing and probably could not happen today. That era of benign neglect in raising children was a gift so rare that we didn't, of course, know it was a gift until we were grown. But it was the way of the world in small-town southern America, and we were just fortunate to be the beneficiaries of a simpler time.

Chapter 3

Our *hard* training paid off when time for the Kingsport Horse Show arrived. The show was one of the larger events in our area, attracting Thoroughbred hunters from all over Tennessee. Squire and I were *not* in their league, and I knew it, but it would be good experience for us both. There was no trainer or teacher (oh yeah, *I* was the trainer—this venture was not connected to the Sullins barn), and my riding abilities were probably not honed to the same degree as the elite hunter riders. Nevertheless, I entered Squire in several Equitation classes and a Hunter Hack class, knowing full well that the competition would be fierce.

An equitation class judges the skill of the rider while a hack class judges the adaptability of the horse. In a hack class the judge wants to see a horse that can not only jump but also perform other tasks in a calm, relaxed manner. I was totally unsuccessful in the equitation classes, which considerably bruised my ego for I felt I had a chance in that category because of past success in other shows. So it was with little hope for a ribbon that we entered the ring for the hack class.

After trotting and cantering both directions, each rider was asked to jump two single-rail jumps down the center of the arena, changing canter lead if necessary for a right turn at the end; hand gallop (a controlled gallop) down the long side; halt at the judge's stand near the end; back up three paces; and calmly walk off on a loose rein. Ha! Not as easy as it sounds. After galloping the long side, there were very few of those fine Thoroughbreds that could come to a clean halt (visualize stopping a race horse on a dime), much less back up and then walk off calmly with a relaxed rein. Squire, being a cow pony with Western training had no problem with the task. None at all.

We jumped the two jumps and with a flying lead change made a smooth right turn. As we approached the end of the ring at a considerable gallop, I whispered "Whoa" under my breath. Good ole Squire skidded to a halt so fast he nearly sat down on his haunches. He quickly backed up three steps, I dropped the reins, and he *sauntered* away. We placed fifth in that class of about fifteen hunters. Had I known better about the proper spacing of strides between jumps (I took only one instead of the required two—something, that because of my lack of training, I considered really cool), we may have done even better. Still, it must have really chapped those lovely riders to have a small cow pony with a roached mane outperform their beautiful Thoroughbreds.

As with all good things that come to an end, the day finally arrived that I must have known would come. Squire was a good horse and had learned his lessons well. Nothing, however, could have prepared me for what took place the day after the Kingsport horseshow. I drove to the barn to give Squire some treats on his well-deserved day off, and as I made my way up the long tree-shaded driveway of the Repass's home, singing along with the radio and feeling that all was right with the world, something unusual caught my eye.

There was a long unfamiliar horse trailer parked next to the barn. My first thought was that a new horse must have just arrived, but as I got closer I saw that the door was *closing* on a newly loaded horse. It was Squire—there was no mistaking that scarred rump of his—and before I could stop my car and get out, the trailer pulled away. I was stunned. Why had no one told me he was for sale? Of course, no one was obligated to tell me a thing. Squire was not my horse, and Four Winds was in the business of buying and selling horses. Nevertheless my heart was having a terrible time grasping that reality.

"What is going on, Cliff?" I asked the barn foreman, my voice quavering. "Where are they taking Squire?"

"Fellow bought him from the doctor last night…needed a horse for his daughter."

I couldn't just stand there and weep in front of the man, so I turned around, got in my car and sped away. Once I was out of sight I pulled over and fell apart. It was a cold and brutal lesson in growing up, and it stung mightily. I had done my job well—perhaps too well. I used to wonder if it would have been easier had I arrived five minutes later and simply not found Squire in his stall, but, of course, I knew better. There was no easy way to let go, but it would have been nice to say goodbye.

In reflection, I know and realize that the generosity of Dr. Repass was remarkable and quite unbelievable. He basically *gave* me a free horse for a year. I never signed any kind of waiver nor did my parents spend a single dime for that horse's care. Complete and utter free rein was mine. Why in the world did he do that? Of course there was never any kind of remuneration for my "training services," so I suppose we both had a sweet deal. I find it hard to understand why my parents were not a part of this nebulous contract, but for a brief period and for *whatever* reason— kismet, kindheartedness or just plain good business—I had a horse that felt like my very own.

Part II

Finding Buzz

What the colt learns in youth he continues in old age.

French Proverb

A horse is the projection of people's dreams about themselves—strong, powerful, beautiful— and it has the capability of giving us escape from our mundane existence, but be wary of the horse with a sense of humor.

Pam Brown, Australian Poet

Chapter 4

My carefree riding days ended when I left for college. Hollins College, a private women's institution in Roanoke, Virginia, had a well-respected riding program that garnered top awards in regional competitions, and I would have given just about anything to be a part of that program. The cost, however, was prohibitive so as a result I was off on new adventures. The opportunity to ride was a rare occurrence, and it took twenty years, marriage and two children before riding again became a part of my life.

My daughter, Tilghman, at age ten, came to me one day and begged for riding lessons (*beg* being the operative word here because nothing about horses is inexpensive). We visited a barn near our home in Bellevue, Washington, to make inquiries, and there in the middle of the aisle at Evergreen Equestrian Center, I was struck by déjà vu. Tears welled in my eyes when I saw and smelled those horses. Every horse memory I possessed came flooding forth.   I knew right away that this venture was going to get *awfully* expensive because I was going to have to take lessons, too.

Tilghman and I were in heaven.   It was terrific sharing a common passion, and I had a ball watching her learn.   Riding styles for hunt-seat riding had changed considerably since my younger days, so I learned new techniques right alongside my budding equestrienne. My earlier riding largely centered on a "seat-of-the-pants" approach—I could make a horse do just about anything I needed it to do.   But my new lessons taught me the more refined compulsory moves that required a new level of connection with the horse that had never been experienced before.   Quickly I learned that I did not know quite as much as I thought I knew.

After three years of riding at Evergreen and having the occasional half-lease on a favorite horse, an opportunity arose to finally buy a horse of my own.   It was June of 1994.   I was *43 years old*.   One gloriously sunny day, as I watched Tilghman take a jumping lesson in the outdoor arena, a pregnant woman rode down the hill from the adjoining equestrian park seeking a buyer for her big 16.3-hand Thoroughbred gelding named Buzz.   This horse, a dark dappled grey with a black mane and salt-and-pepper tail, was a striking, handsome specimen, and all eyes were focused on the two of them as they approached the outdoor arena. The woman, Kelly Mooney, needed to sell Buzz for a variety of reasons so she left him at the barn for any interested person who wished to have a "test drive." A beauty contest of sorts commenced.

It almost felt like a jealous competition for who was most suited to ride this animal. Several people were in the market for a horse at the time, and all were intrigued by Buzz. As most riders know, horses require differing degrees of riding ability, and it was interesting to observe how Buzz related to the various "testers." He was just a bit "hot" for some of the beginning adult riders, and it was beginning to look like he would need an experienced hand.

Tilghman was the exception, however. Her experience level and mine were obviously different— she had only been riding for three years—and even though we possessed two divergent riding styles Buzz responded in kind to both of us in a way that was appropriate to each skill level. It was astounding. We were jumping fences at different heights in our lessons, and he allowed each of us, in our own manner, to ride with confidence and assurance. Buzz seemed to be taking care of Tilghman. Finding such an animal is not easy. Tilghman said to me after a test ride one day, "His gaits are so smooth and steady, and I can see the distances to the jumps so easily. There is no guessing how many strides he will take—it just seems to work out perfectly! And when he lands, it is like landing on a pile of *foam*."

We were smitten. Other riders showed interest in Buzz, but no offers were tendered, so I asked Kelly if we could lease Buzz with first right of refusal should a buyer materialize. Happily for us she agreed, and the appropriate document was drawn up. Having never owned a horse, I was far more comfortable with this arrangement.

Sharing Buzz couldn't have been more perfect. Tilghman and I each rode him three days a week, and on the seventh day he rested. We never argued over when either one of us should ride him or when we should clean his stall. If schedules changed we easily adapted or asked a friend to fill in. There was *never* a paucity of people wanting to ride Buzz. The situation was ideal— one that I still marvel over today. Anyone with middle-school-aged children might not believe that such a situation could exist. But it did.

Chapter 5

Our first horseshow with Buzz drew near, and Tilghman and I entered several classes. It was an "open division" class (a class open to professionals and amateurs) with jumps 2'9"to 3'3" that swiftly changed our leasing status. Upon entering the ring I noticed that the first jump was the only obstacle measuring 2'9." All the rest were 3'3" and they looked *big*. The height of jumps that I usually trained over was 3'. The extra three inches, unbelievably, is a game changer. I had no idea what to expect.

Buzz had just carried Tilghman around a 2'6" course like a seasoned veteran, but these larger jumps were going to require a little more fire. I cannot describe the magic of that round. He soared over every obstacle with inches to spare, his forelegs tucked and ears pricked forward. He had as much fun, it seemed, as I did. We placed second in competition with all those professional riders, and I was thrilled.

More than a few trainers approached my trainer after that ride inquiring about purchasing possibilities. Buzz had made quite an impression, both in my round and Tilghman's. His versatility was evident, so now my hand was called. I had to put up or shut up. If I didn't buy this horse, there were plenty of people who would. The apprehension about the debt I would acquire was overwhelming, but the opportunity was one I could not miss, so a call to Kelly to tell her we wished to purchase her horse set in motion considerable angst and some restless, sleepless nights.

It would take me years to pay off a credit card cash advance on my salary as a piano instructor! Had I even considered his monthly board and vet bills? Good Lord, shoes! He would need to be shod every five weeks or so and would certainly need the very latest in fashionable horse clothing—saddles, bridles, halters— had I lost my mind?

But the very next week on Father's Day, as my husband, Bill, opened his gifts, he said, "Hang on a minute. I have something for you two."

"What in the world, Bill?" I said. "This is *Father's* Day."

"Well, just sit tight while I go get it."

30

He went into his office and came out with a box and a card and placed them on the dining room table where we sat after finishing dinner (I do not recall why my son, Will, was absent). Bill always waits until later in the day to open his birthday presents and the like—a quirk that used to drive our children crazy. Tilghman opened the box, paused to look up at me and said, "Mom!"

"What?"

"Mom!" she repeated with tears forming in her big beautiful eyes.

She handed me the box and therein sat a check that Bill had written for the purchase amount of one Big Blue Buzzard. I was overcome. I had not even *hinted* that I wanted help in buying this horse and out of pride or stubbornness had certainly not asked for such a thing. Buckets of tears ensued. Tilghman and I sobbed, screamed, jumped up and down and showered Bill with hugs and kisses. We were getting a horse!

"This has got to be the best Father's Day I have ever had," said Bill.

Bless his heart; this gift was something much more than generous, loving and beautiful. This gift ultimately launched a journey of love and discovery so rich that it altered many of my beliefs, and, amazingly, it changed my basic outlook on life. The journey continues to shape much of my thinking today, and because it is ongoing and ever-expanding I am finally able to give voice to my story of Buzz.

Buzz and I are at our first horseshow at Bridle Trails State Park while he was still under lease. Just look at those forelegs!
That jump round changed our leasing status. Bunny Coffin, a good friend and highly respected horsewoman told me I would be *crazy* not to buy him.

Tilghman and Big Blue Buzzard get a big blue
ribbon at Bridle Trails State Park.

A proud pair.

Buzz is listening to me (check out his ears). Am I
saying "That's a gooood boy" or sticking my tongue
out like Michael Jordon?

Another shot at a LWSC C-rated show in Bridle Trails
State Park.

Dang…too close, my fault, but Buzz was a
scrambler.

Tilghman entering the ring at Bridle Trails StatePark.

Lots of lovin' after a hard day.

A favorite picture, but due to the camera angle
Buzz's head is *insanely* out of proportion, much
like a fish made to appear enormous when held
closer to the lens.

My efforts on the flat in an Equitation class.

Oops—reins too long, but Buzz is in a lovely frame at a canter.

Buzz and I taking a breather during a jump lesson at
Evergreen Equestrian Center.

Back to work...all eyes on the next jump.

!

Tilghman goofing off in our backyard.

Visiting a neighbor…love that Santa Hat!

Buzz at Evergreen Equestrian Center—his home for three years.

Something has my attention.

Part III

A Unique Bond

*I have often said there's nothing better for the
inside of a man than the outside of a horse.*

Ronald Reagan

*There is something about jumping a horse over
a fence, something that makes you feel good.
Perhaps it's the risk, the gamble. In any event
it's a thing I need.*

William Faulkner

Chapter 6

Big Blue Buzzard was the official registered name on the Jockey Club Thoroughbred certificate of registration. Foaled on April 14, 1987, by Northern Supremo out of Greykeet, Buzz was born a roan (reddish brown) colt. It was surprising to learn this since he was a dark dappled grey when we bought him. Many grey horses are black when born, turning a mixture of black and white as they age, but it amazed me that Buzz was born a roan because there was no hint of brown in his coat.

Bred to be a racehorse, Buzz possessed the tattoo under his upper lip to identify him as such. In researching his lineage, I discovered that his grandfather was Northern Dancer, a famous stocky bay Thoroughbred race horse that held the record for the mile and one quarter distance of the Kentucky Derby (exactly two minutes) from 1964 until 1973 when

Secretariat ran it in 1:59$2/5$...a smokin' $3/5$ second faster. That record still holds today.

Further digging produced an even more interesting genealogy. Northern Dancer's grandfather was Native Dancer, also known as the Grey Ghost. Big, bossy and *grey,* he was hailed, on the front of Time magazine in 1954, as one of the finest Thoroughbred race horses of all time, winning 21 of his 22 starts. It was written:

*The memory of the true champion lives on for generations after the mathematics of his achievement have been forgotten. His epitaph is not the thin type of the record book or the chest full of blackened silver trophies. It is **legend.***

Native Dancer's picture on the magazine cover bears a striking *astonishing* resemblance to his great-great grandson.

Speed, however, was apparently not Buzz's strong suit, so his breeder allowed him to live a happy, unfettered life at pasture until purchased by Kelly, the woman who sold him to us. She trail rode him, did some low-key jumper training and generally gave him a comfortable life.

Kelly told me a funny story, however, about riding Buzz in Bridle Trails Park one evening right before dark. They approached the quarter mile stretch— a straight, unimpeded and wide trail on which many loved to let loose and fly—and Buzz's racehorse legacy apparently came to the fore. She said he bolted as if "out of the gates" and spiritedly tore down that tract faster than he had ever run before. Not able to slow him one whit, he finally stopped on his own when the trail narrowed. "That *never* happened again," Kelly laughed. "I suppose he got it out of his system."

I relate this bit of history because much of his temperament was due to his lack of abuse at the racetrack (excepting that tattoo!). Good training and informal, often bareback, pleasure riding helped shape the remarkably easy attitude. He was, one might say, a Thoroughbred with a warmblood brain (a warmblood is a cross between a cold-blooded draft horse, such as a Percheron or Clydesdale, and a hot-blooded Thoroughbred or Arabian).

Buzz had many traits of his hot-blooded Thoroughbred breeding, but they were tempered by a mellow warmblood sensibility. If Buzz stayed in his stall for more than a day he was like a missile to deal with, but if exercised, he was bombproof on a busy street.

Many people asked if we intended to change his name. I suppose it had a certain unattractive ring to it, but it was a perfect fit in our estimation. He was steel-blue gunmetal grey in color, possessed an overbite that is known as "parrot mouth," and was big, so what could be more fitting than Big Blue Buzzard?

Apparently there was a story behind his naming that I was never able to wrest from the breeder, and naturally that made me more curious than ever, but it really didn't matter because we thought it humorous and apt. We also figured that any judge at a horseshow would probably look up from his or her judging notes when hearing such an unusual name and thus pay closer attention—"And next in the ring is number 53, Tilghman Carroll riding Big Blue Buzzard"—so no new fancy formal name was adopted. Buzz it was and Buzz it stayed.

From the very beginning, Buzz was a force. He had personality writ large—perhaps as large as his considerable stature. When I cleaned stalls in his small auxiliary barn at Evergreen, Buzz would lean out over the guard chain of his open cubicle and tip over the manure cart in the aisle. He would then pick up the broom and swing it about, tossing his head up and down at his antics, and paw the concrete in pure unadulterated horse glee. Anything that wasn't nailed down was fair game—halters, ropes, hats, buckets, blankets—you name it.

Cleaning the five stalls in Buzz's barn helped pay for his boarding costs, and I learned that just as some people are more fastidious than others so are some horses. Whether by training or inherent trait, many horses will eliminate in one corner of their cubicle, making "mucking out" a breeze. Buzz, unfortunately, did not possess that potential gene. He dropped manure *throughout* his stall, then thoroughly and effectively churned, twirled and stirred the mix until every square inch of bedding was soiled. It always looked as if a giant mix master had spent the night. Tilghman and I were sure he reveled in kicking and spreading the manure about before settling down for the night with a fresh soft pile for a pillow.

A brownish green jowl, neck and matted mane, proof of our suspicions, greeted us most mornings. Grooming, as a result, was a bit more time consuming. Because green and brown are more visible on greys than on horses of darker shades, Buzz had to endure vigorous brushing—*not* the favorite part of his day. When secured by cross-tie chains in the barn aisle for grooming, Buzz *rarely* stood still. Even when he was not being scrubbed, Buzz was always in perpetual motion, with lots of ready energy and little regard for anyone's personal space. Those big hooves dancing around on the concrete were a menace to a foot in anything but a sturdy boot, but Buzz was never mean spirited— just thin skinned, ticklish and impatient.

All that being said, Buzz did have a favorite "itch spot." Just like a dog has a tickle zone that will send hind legs into a scratching frenzy, most horses have a favorite spot that elicits groans and grunts of pure pleasure. Buzz's spot was right above his left shoulder on his withers. I came upon it quite accidentally while power-brushing a particularly stubborn manure stain. Scratching that spot sent him into moaning ecstasy. He would hyperextend his neck—canting his head sideways—and grow weak in the knees. His lip would curl up, exposing those protruding buck teeth, and quiver uncontrollably until the scratching stopped. It was a great trick for eliciting a grin from onlookers, and it is hard to say who it tickled more—him, them or me.

Chapter 7

Despite Buzz's display of spirited and sometimes annoying impatience, he revealed that he also had a tender side. An orange barn cat would often make rounds in the barn and pause for a nuzzle in Buzz's feed manger. The cat would rub his head and body against Buzz's muzzle, purring like mad, and then Buzz would exhale making the creature look like he was caught in a wild windstorm. Both animals would have their eyes closed. Seeing such an amazing exchange never failed to charm me. That enormous horse and diminutive cat were best friends.

Buzz's good nature continued to present itself. My friend Diana Berry came by on her horse Barney from a neighboring barn one morning to meet Buzz. While she and Barney stood outside the railing of the outdoor arena, we walked over to say hello. Buzz and Barney touched noses, and just when Diana was beginning to pull back, in case one of them squealed and struck out with a foreleg, Buzz slurped Barney's face from nostril to eye. This unexpected and quite unusual display of affection made us howl with laughter. Tenderness from such a large animal is a delightful thing to behold, and I was quickly learning the ways in which Buzz delighted me.

In a hurry to get to the barn for a trail ride one afternoon, I injured my scalp on an open kitchen cabinet door—the pesky injury incurred when rising to meet a sharp corner—causing me not only to see stars but also to bleed profusely. Not feeling like riding because my head hurt too much, I sat down in Buzz's pasture under a tree to quietly observe his grazing. He made his way over to where I was sitting and started nuzzling my head. Wary that he might try to take a nibble, I readied myself to quickly duck, but to my amazement he inhaled deeply, blew very softly and then tenderly licked my wound. His gentleness almost made me cry.

But as gentle as Buzz sometimes was, he also had a not-so-gentle quirk that *I* happily didn't have to experience! Large-breasted women were not entirely safe around Buzz. Something about large bosoms made him a little crazy. He would invariably reach out to try to steal a bite, and there was more than one report that he landed his target—oh ouch—landing *him* with the moniker Big Blue *Boob-Biting* Buzzard!

Chapter 8

Buzz was a dream to ride. His wonderful gaits and steady approach to jumps inspired confidence. Each time I mounted Buzz, though, a new trick or two were revealed. Some were handy and others were just funny.

One of his handy tricks was holding my riding crop while I readied the saddle for mounting. Before discovering this, I would fumble with the stick while trying to tighten the saddle girth and lower the stirrups. I could never quite decide what to do with it, so one day when Buzz turned his head toward me to see if there might be one more treat coming his way, I gave the crop to him to hold. He happily obliged. Buzz would hold it in his teeth while I prepared the saddle and give it back when I was ready to mount. My trainer always scolded me for that, saying it made him mouthy. But I figured if he was already mouthy why not use it for my benefit!

Mouthy. Exactly what does that mean? Another more descriptive term might be "lippy." Buzz's upper lip was constantly engaged—nudging, kneading and searching for treats. He could smell a carrot the instant you entered the barn, and because he was probably indulged as a baby, he wouldn't stop looking—probing every pocket—until you produced the treat or tied him up! I loved that crazy lip, though. It was certainly a trademark.

Further up his lip, between his nostrils, the skin was a pale, pale pink that turned a deeper sunburned pink in the summer (sunblock was once considered). The skin, soft as a lamb's ear, was extremely kissable. I cannot count the times I opened his stall door to see a bright, vivid lipstick imprint smack between his nostrils. Reminding me of the ubiquitous World War II graffiti cartoon "Kilroy Was Here" which was mysteriously found or left behind by our advancing troops, those kissing lips were Tilghman's stealth signature.

But as far as tricks…a particularly funny one occurred after a lesson on a hot day. We were walking along the arena perimeter, having just finished a course of jumps, when Buzz decided to scratch his sweaty, itchy ear. Many horses do this by rubbing their heads on their foreleg or a post, but Buzz had a better way. He scratched his ear with his hind leg! Imagine my surprise, sitting astride him, when I saw this *huge* left haunch come around my leg while he lowered his head to scratch his ear with a shod hoof, exactly as a dog would do. I half-expected him to sit down to finish the task, and I can assure you that everybody in the barn was cracking up.

Those sweaty, itchy ears were marvelous. The backs of them, seen only when riding him, were nearly black with white marble veining that resembled the markings of a zebra. They were, excepting that silken nose, Tilghman's favorite thing. I loved them too. When I rode Buzz, his ears were in constant motion— perking forward to assess a distraction, cocking back to listen to my chatter, perking forward again to focus on a jump and then back to me to receive my praise. Often, one was forward and the other one backward, making sure he didn't miss a thing! Rarely did I see them laid fully back in anger or warning. He saved that display for fellow horses in the field that tried to bully or bite him.

Buzz's all-time best trick happened one day when riding with Teri Duplass, my trainer. This trick was both handy and funny. After a few laps around the arena, no matter what the weather, I always got too warm and removed my jacket. A quick toss landed it on a jump standard without fail. Teri, on the other hand, would invariably miss the target, and her jacket would fall on the ground. It became a standing (no pun intended) joke between us. One day, though, I missed the mark and my jacket hit the dust. Teri laughed with raucous delight until Buzz reached down, picked up my jacket in his teeth and dropped it on the jump standard. Oh that *mouthy* beast! Who had the last laugh now? Buzz was making quite a reputation for himself—funny, clever and ever the clown.

Chapter 9

Show season with Buzz was always a
tremendous pleasure. The barn where he boarded
abutted Bridle Trails State Park, an equestrian park
boasting twenty-eight miles of trails and nearly 500
acres of forest. In this gem of a piece of real estate in
the Seattle/Bellevue area is a horseshow venue unlike
any other I've seen. A grand arena with bleachers,
picnic tables and various park facilities sits in the middle
of this forested park with a green canopy of Douglas
firs, cedars, maples and alders creating an atmosphere of
incredible beauty. The majesty of those towering trees,
over a hundred feet high, is a magnificent splendor that
begs description.

Bridle Trails State Park has been state owned
since 1880, but much of its maintenance and upkeep
today is funded by the Lake Washington Saddle Club.
The club, consisting of a dedicated group of volunteers
and a state-funded park ranger, has been supporting

Bridle Trails State Park since 1945. One of its principal means of fundraising is playing host, in the spring and summer, to horseshows in three riding disciplines: English (hunter/jumper), Dressage and Western. Tilghman and I particularly enjoyed the hunter and dressage shows.

Beginning in May, the Saddle Club sponsors several English "fun shows" and two AHSA (American Horse Show Association) "C"-rated hunter shows that are more formal. The "fun shows" provided a great opportunity for getting our feet wet with showing. They were informal and *fun*. Participants were not required to wear hunt coats or braid their horse's mane, and most of the competitors were from our barn, along with a sprinkling of local residents. The "C"-rated shows, however, were more serious in nature. One dressed up, braided the horse's mane and experienced a wider range of competition from area barns.

Buzz seemed to know the difference. If there was ever a time that he was going to misbehave or be a little sloppy, it was at a "fun show." But give him a bath, braid that mane and trim those fetlocks, and Buzz would perform. My mother always told me as a little girl, "Pretty is as pretty does," but Buzz reversed that adage. "Pretty does as pretty is" was his credo, and he rarely failed to adhere to that philosophy at show time. Buzz knew he looked handsome when clean and braided, and handsome he was.

As with clothes that look better on the body than on the hanger, so it was with Buzz "under saddle." Many large horses tend to look ungainly when at rest, but are quite striking when saddled. While Buzz was far from inelegant in his birthday suit—in fact, his conformation, in my eyes, was quite good—his tack definitely enhanced his looks. He was big boned (again more like a warmblood than a Thoroughbred) with a fairly long back and muscular hindquarters, a strong neck that was not at all beefy and a broad chest. If there was any part of him that was less than perfect, it was his head. It was quite large and had, at times, a somewhat goofy air about it. His parrot mouth was partly to blame, but the large white space between his eyes didn't help. Put a handsome bridle on him, though, and that silly look magically disappeared. He looked damn good in his gear and I loved showing him off.

Chapter 10

Tilghman had the honor of riding Buzz in his first horseshow away from home on Bainbridge Island. Unlike the "fun shows" in the park, which were a ten-minute trail ride from our barn, the Bainbridge show necessitated travel in a large horse van to the island via ferryboat. Being novice horse show participants, we had none of the proper traveling accoutrements. How do I even begin to catalogue all that was needed? All the show veterans had show trunks for storing their tack and grooming gear. We did not.

Fortunately, I came across one belonging to the owner of our barn that had been tossed as junk. It was in pretty bad shape, but with a little Yankee ingenuity or perhaps Southern resourcefulness I was able to find a man who was adept at refurbishing wood and metal. With paint and a lot of elbow grease, the trunk turned out to be quite presentable. It even bore a monogram with two of Tilghman's and my initials.

Next on the list of necessities were leg wraps to protect Buzz's very valuable limbs while traveling. These were thick, quilted pads that covered his lower legs and were secured by several yards of elastic wrap. Buzz's wraps were red, and because that is my favorite color, his blanket and plaid summer sheet were of that hue as well. No other color would suffice, and besides, grey horses do look snazzy in red.

It was his and our first experience of jumping on grass so Buzz had to have a special set of shoes (oh my *smoking* credit card) that used metal caulks or studs to keep him from slipping if the grass was wet. These caulks had to be screwed in each morning and removed each evening. It took a ridiculous amount of time to accomplish this task, and it required special equipment as well. Once the caulks were taken out, the holes had to be packed with a special oiled batting material and rubber plugs to keep the screw threads clean. The following morning, the plugs and packing were removed, and the process was repeated. Good heavens, it was back-breaking work. I marvel that farriers are able to work as long as they do.

Our most time consuming task was braiding Buzz's mane. Wake-up call was around 5:00 a.m. As I mentioned earlier, Buzz didn't like to stand still in the crossties, so Tilghman and I braided while he ate his breakfast. Through bleary eyes and dim light we began our task with Tilghman starting at one end and I the other. Standing on overturned buckets, the two of us could get the job done in ninety minutes or so.

A proper braid for a hunter show is a thing of beauty and is not easy to make. The mane is about four or five inches long, (a tedious chore in itself requiring constant upkeep)—which is standard for this discipline—so the braid is quite small. There are usually about twenty-five to thirty braids in the end result, and the process is exacting. It starts with an inch-wide section of mane moistened with water. The rest of the process is achieved in as many different ways as there are Carter's Little Liver Pills, but we used the accepted method of hunter show braiders in our area.

This required about a foot-long piece of yarn that was folded in half and plaited into the braid. Figuring out how to accomplish this task took several tries, but we finally decided to insert the yarn with the two outer strands of mane near the beginning of the braid. At the end of the braid we took the two trailing pieces of yarn, wrapped them in a loop around the tail end and pulled them through to make a knot. We braided the whole mane in this fashion, and the fact that we ended up in the center with no leftover mane (remember, Tilghman started at one end and I the other) was truly not unlike the joining of two sections of a bridge over water and having it fit precisely in the middle!

But having accomplished this task, we were only halfway through the process. Buzz, however, was finished with breakfast and ready to twirl around his stall. We tied him up, "borrowed" a bit more food from the larder and wondered how fat he was going to be by the end of the show. To complete the braids (is it light outside yet?), we inserted a pull-through gadget, similar to a crochet hook, into each braid at the base of the mane. By catching the trailing yarn underneath and pulling it through the top of the braid, we formed a loop. The yarn, now lying across the other side of Buzz's neck, *of course,* tickled the p-double o-p out of him, and the twitching began.

After the entire mane was "pulled through," the tying off began. Tilghman was far better than I at tying off, and I was far better at keeping Buzz's attention off his crazed twitching, so teamwork was the order of the day. To tie off, the yarn was brought forward under the looped braid and tied into a knot. Then the yarn was crossed over the top of the braid about one-third of the way down the loop and tied into a double knot, flattening the braid against the neck as close to the base of the mane as possible and creating a little bump at the top of the braid. An end result that is uniform and straight is almost impossible unless you are a pro, but Tilghman's handiwork came pretty close to *almost* perfect.

Finding a word to describe the resulting braid is difficult—perhaps a squished baseball-park peanut or the number 8. The forelock required a little different method in that Tilghman had to French-braid the first half before finishing off in the regular fashion. This required a gross of carrots to keep Buzz still because a head butt could send Tilghman flying off that bucket.

The whole procedure was, naturally, reversed at the end of the day (just like the shoe caulks) because, heaven forbid, if the braids were left in, Buzz would scratch and rub all night and ruin his mane. I should mention that unbraiding required a seam ripper and about an hour's worth of time, and I probably should not forget to say that we had to repeat this process every morning of the show.

We could have hired someone to do all of this for us, but our budget did not allow such luxury. If the truth be known we had a wonderful time with each other doing the job, and Tilghman also felt the pride and sense of accomplishment that comes with doing the work.

Chapter 11

Doing the work is an understatement. With Tilghman being the principal rider at the Bainbridge Island show, I was the principal "show Mom." I had sorely underestimated the value of this role. In fact, I had probably even judged these mothers as a *bit* overbearing or obsessed. Little did I know how important or, more correctly, abused they are.

I ran around the entire day with a towel hanging from my belt and a bucket with show necessities (hoof pick, hoof polish, body brush, tail brush, show sheen, sticky glide stuff that helps the rider stay in the saddle) and lots of elbow grease. In addition to keeping both horse and rider spotless, I served as water girl. I carried a water bottle for both Tilghman *and* Buzz, and in keeping with all the tricks he could perform, Buzz would even drink out of a plastic cup if Tilghman, sitting on his back, pulled his head around with the rein and poured the water into his mouth . All the other horses drank out of a bucket!

Of course, my principal role as "show Mom" was cheerleader, and there was no equal in that department. I can yell and cheer louder and better than just about anybody alive and Tilghman and Buzz's performance gave me much reason to do so. It was a terrific experience for all of us, and I cannot remember ever being so tired when it was all over. I don't even recall the ribbon placements she won, nor is it important. They performed beautifully, they were gorgeous, and I could not have been more proud.

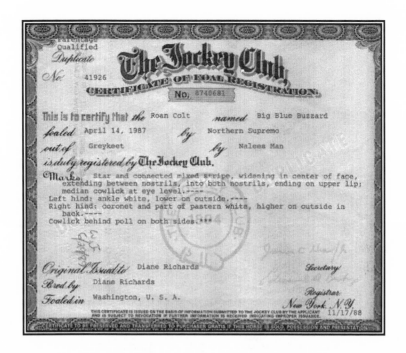

Buzz's certificate of Thoroughbred registration.

Buzz's grandfather Northern Dancer held the
Kentucky Derby record for nine years...2 minutes
flat.

73

TIME
THE WEEKLY NEWSMAGAZINE

NATIVE DANCER
A little heartbreak, then a burst of glory.

Buzz's great-great-grandfather, Native Dancer, was hailed in 1954 as the Greatest Horse of the Year. The resemblance of Buzz to his distant sire is uncanny.

Buzz as a baby with the breeder's granddaughter and his dam Greykeet. The breeder obviously had tremendous trust in Buzz's mommy. He inherited her DNA...his *brown* coat amazes me, though!

75

Tilghman and Buzz at the Bainbridge
horseshow…the first time on grass.

Entering the arena at Bainbridge. Buzz is checking out the jumps.

Hanging out in a Northwest drizzle.

Part IV

Discovery

Ride the horse in the direction that it's going.

Werner Erhard, critical thinker

Chapter 12

The close partnership with Tilghman began to change as she grew older. Once she was able to drive a car, a whole new life opened up for her and riding held lesser sway. Of course she loved Buzz, but his primary care fell to me.

There were many horseshows and many trail rides, many lessons and many laughs, but an injury to Buzz before my biggest dream horseshow became the catalyst that began a journey of transformation and the shifting of my ideology. This injury and the ensuing experiences related to its healing initiated my sharing this story.

The Evergreen Classic Horse Show, which took place at Marymoor Park in Redmond, Washington, was a glorious affair. As an "A"-rated AHSA show, it attracted top hunter/jumper riders from all along the West Coast and Canada and was this hunter rider's long-time goal. To have a horse that was good enough to compete with some mighty fine, expensive and amazingly beautiful horseflesh was a thrill, and after two years of training and hard work, Buzz and I were ready. We were so ready.

One week before the show, I brought Buzz out of his stall and discovered a huge swelling, about the size of a large grapefruit, on his left front knee. My heart sank. The vet was called immediately, and he administered the appropriate medications. He said I should be able to get back in the saddle in three days. I hosed the leg with cold water, wrapped it with ice and waited.

After the three days, I longed him—put him through the paces on a long lead line—and he showed no ill effects. He looked great. But when I mounted him and started to trot, there was a stutter step from behind—a missed cadence—that for some reason did not translate to the canter. His trot was the only gait affected. Back on the longe line he was stutter-step free. My instant intuitive and intelligent deduction was that he had hurt his back in some manner when he had hurt his left knee, but the vet, finding no evidence of pain, was not so sure. He prescribed more bute (phenylbutazone—the horse equivalent of ibuprofen) and the condition improved—somewhat.

A quick digression is in order to describe how one administers bute to a horse. The *large* pill—I now understand the nascency of the term "horse pill"—must be ground into a powder and mixed into his grain. No matter how well it is ground or how well it is mixed, the horse tastes its bitterness in his feed and will avoid eating it. Oh sure, he might eat it once and maybe even twice, but forget about it after that. I used molasses and any manner of goodies to mask the flavor and bind it to his grain, but I always found a good deal of the powdered dinner staring at me in his manger. But the horseshow was looming large, and Buzz *was* improving, even on partial doses. He finally appeared pain free on the bute so, with our vet's approval, we headed for Marymoor Park and the Evergreen Classic.

I cannot begin to describe how excited I was to be entering this venue. For this show, the grounds of the park were transformed into a veritable fantasyland. There were multiple arenas set up for the different categories of jumpers, with the grandest site being the Grand Prix arena. The size of the jumps (four feet and above) was astonishing, and the creative arrangement of obstacles with plants and beautiful flowers was equally amazing. I was more than content, *thank you very much,* to be relegated to the Adult Amateur arena where the jumps were three feet in height.

For those who do not ride, a three-foot jump can also be made to appear, in my estimation, quite enormous with roll tops, oxers (a jump with two or three rails spaced in ascending height), horizontal ladders, brightly painted barrels and coops full of flowers or various other things to make a horse think twice before committing to leap over. The jumps may not only be three-feet high, but the spread may be three-feet wide as well. A woman my age had little business going over these jumps to begin with, but the sheer fun of it on Buzz made the danger less threatening.

Danger, of course, is a given component in horseback riding. It is something one must weigh when making the decision to ride, especially as an adult. As a child, though, danger never entered my mind...at least not until my senior year in high school.

Chapter 13

It was right before the spring horseshow at Sullins College that danger made itself known. I was jumping a practice round on the course in the field, and my school horse, Goldbrick, an enormous pale gold Palomino, made the jumps seem like Tinker Toys. After taking the initial brush jump out of the ring, we angled right in order to negotiate a wide left turn to a large log hurdle. Upon clearing the logs, we headed for an imitation brick wall. Suddenly, for no apparent reason, a stride before the obstacle, Goldbrick took a massive gasp of air, heaved forward and hit the jump with his forelegs. The action flipped him and me a full 180 degrees over the jump with me hitting the ground first. I skidded a few feet past the wall and remember a strange dreamlike sensation of sliding under water along the ocean floor—in ultra-slow motion—and then shouts and cries I could not understand.

The ground shook as Goldbrick fell with a mighty thud. By good fortune or divine intervention, he landed at my side instead of on top of me—which appeared inevitable to witnesses standing by. Only able to glance over when he lifted his head with an agonizing groan, I watched in shock as he fell dead. Scores of people rushed to my aid, but little could be done to console my grief. The consensus, absent an autopsy, was that Goldbrick had suffered a heart attack. It was the only thing that made sense, given the chain of events.

Though not seriously injured—a doctor's visit confirmed no hip fracture—I was badly bruised, physically and psychologically. Somehow I managed to ride that jump course in the horseshow two days later (get *back* in the saddle, young lady) with right much pain and plenty of fear in my heart. The name of the horse I rode that day escapes me—I had never been on his back—but Barbara, my long-time instructor, assured me he was steady and sure and insisted I conquer my fear.

I cannot remember—ever—being so afraid, but I do vividly remember the last three jumps of that course. Coming downhill to a two-jump line (we had

86

successfully negotiated the brick wall that had spelled such disaster earlier), I essentially stopped riding. Actually I *closed* my eyes, held on and prayed any prayer I could muster. "Please just let me finish. Please keep me in this saddle." My horse, sensing my absence of purpose, took full advantage and ran out on the second jump. Fortunately the latter prayer to keep me in the saddle was answered when inertia failed in its objective to send me flying over the jump solo. Eyes now wide open, I luckily stayed with my horse and circled around to take the second jump to complete the line. We then headed across the field to the final obstacle, and my first prayer was granted when we cleared it without mishap. Upon landing, I burst into tears.

I had no control. I sobbed. I cried on so many levels—relief that I finished unscathed, mad that I had given up on the downhill line, and deeply saddened by the death of Goldbrick, a grand horse. Barbara ran over to me, patted me on the leg, smiled broadly and said, "Good job, Lean. See...I knew you could do it. Now stop that blubbering and get on back to the barn." Twenty-two years elapsed before I ever again looked at another jump.

Chapter 14

When I started riding again with Tilghman, it took quite some time for my confidence in going *over* obstacles, instead of around them, to experience a rebirth. My new riding skills gave me a better understanding for proper pacing and judgment of distances, but my past experience gave me a healthy dose of caution in their execution. That being said, however, by the time Buzz and I headed to the Evergreen Classic horseshow, he had earned my absolute confidence as my partner—whether in the ring or on the trails. Several incidents brought about this trust, but the following episodes are a few of my favorites.

One morning, a new employee of our barn and I decided to go for a trail ride. From the barn, we walked up the hill on the graveled road toward Bridle Trails Park, and right before the entrance to the park, something spooked Buzz. I was, stupidly, relaxed and turned sideways in the saddle, chatting with my companion, when Buzz made a swift 180-degree turn and dashed down the hill. The quick departure left me flat on my back, head pointing downhill and the wind knocked out of me, wondering what had happened.

As my breathing slowly returned, I lay cursing—vowing to send Buzz to the dog-food factory—when, to my ever-enduring surprise, he came back up that hill. When a horse runs back to the barn, you may as well kiss him goodbye. You will find him back in his stall happily munching his hay. But Buzz turned and *came back* to me. He stood a few feet away hanging his head close to the ground and looking awfully contrite (he knew he was in trouble), but I could only laugh and marvel at what he had just done. The young woman riding with me concurred that she had never witnessed such a thing. It was the first and last time Buzz ever intentionally off-loaded me.

A second occasion of trust-building occurred when jumping in the indoor arena at our barn. Buzz and I were coming across the ring on a diagonal line to a three-foot oxer in the center. Upon landing after the jump, my weight shifted into my right heel to encourage Buzz to stay right as we approached the end of the arena. But the stirrup leather broke the instant he touched the ground, giving me the sensation of stepping into an empty elevator shaft.

We were approaching the corner, and bad trouble reared its head. Trying my best to hang on, I slid downward to the right and yanked Buzz in the mouth since the reins were my only means of purchase. At the same time, the loose stirrup bounced into his belly with each stride.

Any normal horse, and certainly any Thoroughbred, would have taken off like a scalded cat, leaving me plastered to the wall, but Buzz did not. In fact, he slowed down, rounded the corner and made an indescribable bounce motion, almost as if he were trying to get under me. That strange move kept me hanging on, and then Buzz stopped dead still. *Dead still.* I hauled myself back into the saddle as I hate to hit the ground and observed more than a few dropped jaws among those who witnessed the event. Teri, shaking her head and muttering something about Buzz being worth his weight in gold, brought in a new stirrup leather and insisted we take the jump again. I resisted but ultimately (despite a pounding heart and trembling limbs) complied, and we nailed it. And Buzz nailed my heart to his forever after.

A similar thing occurred when jumping in the new outdoor arena at the neighboring barn. The ring has a very slight incline that is scarcely noticeable, except when it has been raining. The footing becomes wetter in the lower end, and caution must be used.

Buzz and I were there to take a lesson with a local professional jumping coach. As we finished our course, heading downhill to the last line of two jumps, we approached the corner. It was during our turn when all hell broke loose. Buzz first stumbled to his knees, nearly pitching me onto the railing. He recovered, only to then have all four legs slide out from under him. He fell hard on his left side. Miraculously I had stayed on him, but was now partially under him. A sudden realization of imminent doom was followed by a quick prayer. This was *not good!* But Buzz immediately scrambled to his feet, relieving me of his sizable bulk. Nonetheless, all was not well.

My foot was caught in the stirrup, and because Buzz was so big I was hanging with only my upper torso touching the ground. Several scenarios come to mind when considering what Buzz could have done. None of them are pleasant. But Buzz just stood there. He did not budge. The trainer quietly walked over, took hold of the reins, and after some maneuvering helped me get my foot out of the stirrup. He told me what I already knew. He told me I was lucky to have such a wonderful horse.

Chapter 15

But back to the Evergreen Classic! A curiosity at large horse shows is the configuration of portable stalls. Each competing barn secures a block of stalls before the show. To store food and bedding, there are always several more units rented than the number needed for the horses coming. But the novelty lies in how a couple of stalls are transformed into the tack rooms and "living areas."

The amount of work and money that goes into the creation of these spaces is astonishing. The wealthier barns bring awnings, sod, bricks, plants, trees, beautiful flowers, *fountains*, mulch and outdoor furniture that is ridiculously fine. The specialty canvas drapes with barn logos emblazoned across the top are gorgeous. On each stall door, there is a wooden or metal plaque with the horse's names engraved on a brass plate. Lots of grooms and barn workers run around raking up errant stalks of hay. The riders use golf carts or small mopeds to ferry back and forth between the stalls and arenas (a fair distance to be sure), with several requisite snarling Jack Russell terriers in tow. And the trainers and riders use walkie-talkies to communicate.

Our barn was not in the league of these super barns. We cleaned and bedded our own stalls, walked or ran back and forth between stalls and arenas to communicate (we finally got smart and brought bikes and walkie-talkies), and certainly made a comfortable and quite presentable space for ourselves that served our purposes. But we undeniably admired and enjoyed the beauty and luxury of the others.

After arriving and getting Buzz situated in his stall, I made my way to the show office to confirm my class list and get my number. Soon afterwards, with much anticipation, I hopped in the saddle to get Buzz and myself used to the hustle and bustle, starting a slow warm-up to see how he was doing. The stutter-step had returned. Please, no. I pushed on in hopes it was simple soreness that would get better after his muscles warmed up, but it did not get better. I asked our vet who was fortunately present to observe us, but he could see no reason to stop. We cantered a few jumps; his canter stride was not affected and jumping was smooth. I continued to canter about for a few more minutes and then took him back to his stall for a rest.

Later that morning, I scheduled a practice round in one of the arenas. The round would give us a chance to take a trial run over the jumps that would be in our classes. I knew the proof of his soundness or lack thereof would be in this round. My fingers were crossed. When it was our turn to go, we entered the ring and rode around the obstacles to get a good look. We headed for the first jump in a line, and Buzz took it perfectly. The second jump was not as good. He took an extra stride, which was not his usual *m.o.*, and a red flag popped in my head.

We jumped another line, which was slightly better, then turned and headed across the diagonal to an impressive oxer. Buzz gathered himself to take the jump, but he put on the brakes one-half stride into it. Poles and standards were falling all around us, and, due to the refusal, I was close to being on top of his head. I can't remember Buzz ever refusing to jump *anything*.

We carefully extricated ourselves from the yard-sale of a mess we had made, waited for the jump to be rebuilt and tried again. Again...dead refusal. My gut was telling me to stop right away and go home, but my trainer Teri *and* my experience were telling me to go at it one more time. I was fully aware that I might be a bit reticent in urging him forward because of his stutter-step, but I knew I had to be sure. Besides, I had been taught it is not wise to let a horse refuse a jump without making him jump *it* or another like it. It had something to do with not letting a 1200-pound horse have the upper hand.

I gathered him up, cantered a small circle and headed for a third time to the oxer. A solid crack of my whip on the flank was incorporated this time, and he jumped—sort of. He hesitated at the base, leapt straight up like a deer and landed nearly flat footed, crashing the last rail down with his hind legs. I think he snapped the rail in two, and his action nearly snapped my neck and back with it. I was seeing stars with that landing, but felt considerable guilt for forcing him to follow my command.

One look at Teri told her that no matter what the vet or *anybody* else said, this horse had an injury that was not healed and we were going home. Teri checked his legs to make sure he hadn't cut himself, and we exited the ring. I wept, just short of wailing, all the way back to the stall. My dream of showing Buzz with the likes of all those other handsome horses was shot. But much worse than that, my beloved horse was still hurting and I didn't know where.

Chapter 16

Actually I *did* know where, but I'm not exactly sure how I knew. As I said earlier, my intuition told me he had hurt his back in some way when he hurt his knee. It only made sense. He didn't have the stutter-step when he was on the longe line. He did have the stutter-step when I was on his back. It didn't seem like rocket science to me, but no vet would concur with my assessment.

My thought was that he had possibly become cast in his stall. This occurs when a horse lies down to roll and finds himself in a position next to the wall, unable to get up—somewhat akin to a turtle on his back—and at times requires human intervention to be righted. Perhaps in his thrashing to get up, he had not only banged his knee against the wall but had also sprained his back.

The vets—notice the plural here—agreed it was a possibility, but saw no proof of any pain upon inspection, so they didn't think it was his actual problem. One vet suspected it was an issue with his hocks; another, the stifle (this is the joint high on the back leg near the flank—corresponding to our knee). Treatment went so far as injecting a type of acid into the stifle to blister the joint, the reason for which I have no memory, but I do remember that it hurt and burned Buzz and took days to heal, for absolutely naught.

Shoes were another consideration. A specialized farrier concluded his problem was pronation and inserted rubber wedges between hoof and shoe. Jutting molars that are sharp and spiky can affect a horse's soundness, so an equine dentist filed and filed away. Next up was a chiropractor. Chiropractors are a legitimate and oft-used practitioner in the horse world— two steps ahead of voodoo and magnets—and I *have* seen horses improve greatly after treatments. But when the man claimed that Buzz's problem was castration tension *(oh come on*—he had only been castrated for almost twelve years now) I decided to discontinue the treatments.

None of this did anything except lighten my bank account. I was convinced, more than ever, that the problem was deep in his back and begged for someone to treat it.

That someone turned out to be a young vet-turned-acupuncturist. This young man, a graduate of Cornell, one of the nation's best vet schools, told me a story of a class he took with a visiting Chinese acupuncturist. That class changed his life. He went to China to study with this man and came back with a new direction for his practice of veterinary medicine, *plus* a bald head, except for a long plait down his back and a Fu Manchu mustache of extraordinary length. A New York Yankees baseball cap jarred the picture, somewhat, of this Zen/Taoist practitioner (my description, not his), but he was all serious business as he set to work.

The needles he used, encased in a plastic tube, were about eight inches long and gossamer thin, and the process he used to insert them was astonishing. Visualize Buzz in the crossties, fidgeting and moving about, and the acupuncturist plying his trade. He first ran his hands along Buzz's back, hovering about two inches above the spine, and stopped where he felt heat. That heat was right behind where the saddle lies. Indeed, he affirmed, there was something there. Applying pressure with his thumb and then his fist didn't seem to get much of a pain response (ergo the lack of evidence of back injury to the other vets), but the heat was definitely there. He told me to hold Buzz as still as possible while he inserted the needles.

Starting with two at the warm spot on his back, he put the plastic tube, with the needle sticking about a half- inch out of the top, on the assigned spot and then tapped the top of the needle until it was flush with the tube. He then removed the tube and proceeded to twist and twirl that needle until it was embedded in the muscle about three or four inches. Yikes! Buzz didn't even flinch.

Next, he needed to tap an opposing meridian that was apparently in the middle of Buzz's forehead right above his eyes. I was a bit dubious, knowing Buzz, but what could I say? He stood right in front of Buzz and attempted to apply the needle. *No way, Jose,* was Buzz having any of that. He flung his head as high as the crossties would allow and sent needle and practitioner flying. Brave soul that he was, the young man tried a second time, but there was not going to be a needle in Buzz's forehead. Period.

The closest second-choice meridian was his chest, and that application was a success. Several more needles were inserted in other places—near his withers, on his shoulder and on his barrel near his front leg—and then we waited. Normally the whole process makes a horse very calm—almost like he is sedated—but not so with Buzz. He tap-danced for the next twenty minutes, not because the needles were hurting, but simply because that is what Buzz did. So this interesting, smart and very honest young man finally admitted that Buzz was probably not a good candidate for acupuncture and that further treatment would be a waste of money and time. He left me with some very strong-smelling herbal liniment that had Chinese characters written all over the bottle and wished me good luck. Luck, it seemed, was certainly what I needed, and that luck arrived in the advice of a friend.

Chapter 17

"Call a horse psychic," said my friend, Lynda Cushman. A who? A what? You cannot be *serious*, I thought. But serious she was.

"Have you ever called one? Do you know one?" I asked.

"Yes! Do you want to hear my story?"

"Tell me *every* detail, Lynda" I enthused.

"Well, our warmblood stallion Kronprinz was acting very lethargic and out of sorts, and our vet was a little puzzled. He could find nothing wrong with him at all. I finally decided to call this woman that somebody told me about, and *she* discovered he was irritated because he wasn't getting alfalfa hay anymore!"

"Oh *sure*, Lynda."

"No, seriously! We had run out of alfalfa and could only get timothy hay from our feed guy. KP was *not* happy. I immediately started looking around for alfalfa and finally found a supplier that could help us. It did the trick, I tell you. KP is a happy camper again. He tore into that first flake of hay like it was candy."

Lynda went on to describe how the psychic had also talked to her pony Twinkle.

"Her description of the pony was exact," Lynda said. "She even said that Twinkle looked so sweet bobbing and weaving in his stall. I really didn't think too much about that", she continued, "until Caitlin [Lynda's daughter] came in later from the barn commenting that Twinkle was acting a little strange...weaving back and forth. She had never seen him do that, ever."

Well, of course, I got all of the contact information. The story was compelling enough that I decided it was worth a try, if for no other reason than it would be a kick in the pants. I was so frustrated with three vets, a specialized farrier, equine dentist, chiropractor and an acupuncturist being unable to help Buzz, that I was ready to try just about anything. I had read that the foremost hunter trainer in the U.S., George Morris, was coerced, against his will, into using a psychic for a problem horse and that the results were smashing. If he, the most respected and conservative horseman alive, achieved results, then, boy howdy, I was willing to give it a go.

I must confess that I am the sort of person who is open to such an idea. The concept of a guardian angel sitting on my shoulder while riding had already be incorporated (she divulged her name to me on an airplane once—*Ethel*—bless her for all those countless times she saved my bacon). The possibility of UFOs and the notion that there is a friendly ghost living in my ancestral home back in Virginia—both are theories that delight and intrigue me. But being a somewhat guarded Southern conservative, did I actually *believe* in the veracity of an animal psychic?

Truly the idea of calling a woman in California, while I sat in my kitchen in Bellevue, Washington, and asking her to communicate with my horse in his stall at a barn three miles from my kitchen was stretching it. Just a bit. But herein lies the stuff that began changing my life, my belief system and my understanding of my world. Herein lie the bones of this story.

Chapter 18

I made that call, and this is what happened. Jeri, the psychic, asked me to tell her five things about Buzz.

"Lean, I need to know your horse's name, age, color, breed and current residence, and by that I mean does he live in a stall or out in a pasture?"

I gave her the information and then said to her, "Jeri, I want to know how Buzz injured himself, where he is hurting and what I can do to help him. I also want to know if he is happy. He has been trying to bite me a lot lately, and I'd like to know why. It would be nice to know if he is happy with Tilghman and me as his owners."

Jeri noted my questions and then said, "I will be presenting myself to Buzz as if I were you. You will hear papers rustling as I collect the information, as I will be in a meditative state while communicating with him. So do *not* hang up." I really did not understand why she would present herself as me, but in the interest of time (and money) I didn't ask.

No more information about who I was or where Buzz was boarded was exchanged. So Jeri began, and I waited. I ran a load of wash, filled the dishwasher, swept the kitchen floor and then sat, tapping my foot. The night before this call, I put Buzz in his stall, kissed him on the nose, and told him that someone was going to be talking to him the next day. I reminded him to be a gentleman. Horse lovers do that sort of thing!

Finally, after about thirty minutes, Jeri came back to the phone, and she was chuckling—*really* chuckling.

"What is so funny?" I asked.

"Buzz is truly a very funny horse. The first thing he did, while standing there in his stall wearing his red quilted blanket was to say, 'Oh hi, I was expecting you!'"

Okaaay, at that moment I began hearing the Twilight Zone theme song, and the little hairs on the back of my neck started to perk up. I thought, perhaps, that she had ascertained from our time chatting that I was gregarious and by extension Buzz was probably outgoing as well, but how did she know he was in a red *quilted* blanket?

"He told me his back was hurting—two vertebrae behind where your 17-inch saddle rests—and that he hurt it while goofing off in the paddock outside. He was bucking and twirling around and fell hard on his left front knee, vaulting hind end over head, nearly breaking his neck. He told me that he badly wrenched his back in the process."

Most saddles are 16 ½-inch but mine is a 17-inch, and isn't that exactly where the acupuncturist detected heat?

"He said that massage would probably help, and time off, too. With regard to the biting, he pointed out that he, in fact, has never hurt you, he is just trying to get your attention. His back is hurting! 'And by the way,' he said, 'I really miss that orange cat. That cat was the king of barn cats and I really miss it. And I miss the black dog—I think it was a Lab—with the white chest. Where are they?' "

At this point, I nearly fell off the kitchen chair. That cat and dog belonged to Teri, my trainer. She and the pets had moved to start their own riding establishment three months prior to this call. I have already said how much Buzz loved that cat. Jeri continued by adding that Buzz really wanted to go swimming and foxhunting. I started to shiver at this point because on a vacation the summer of his accident, Tilghman and I had gone bareback riding in the ocean in Georgia. I told all my riding buddies how fun it was swimming on horseback. And the winter before, I was offered a chance to go foxhunting with a group at the barn next door and griped to my riding buddies that my husband, Bill, did not want me to go because of the perceived danger. All these conversations took place while I was on Buzz's back.

As for whether or not he was happy, Jeri said the following: "Buzz said that he loves being your horse— that the three of you have so much fun together, and nothing is ever too serious. He added he hoped to ride into the sunset with you as his owners."

Boiler-plate "psychic talk" I thought, but she expanded that last comment by saying, "Buzz, however, is missing Tilghman. He says he is afraid of being discarded. What could he mean by that?"

As I mentioned earlier, Tilghman was now a busy high-school senior and had been riding less. She had plenty on her plate with college applications, cross-country running, schoolwork, community service and a busy social life.

I was beginning to feel somewhat—just a titch—off my center! No, I was feeling a *lot* off my center. How could Jeri possibly know these things? How could she *see* him?

"Jeri," I said, "how can you be communicating with Buzz in such human vernacular? His brain is the size of a small grapefruit, and although funny and clever he's still not all that smart."

"Lean, I am not communicating with his brain. I am communicating with his spirit! Every living thing has energy and that energy, whether you call it a spirit or a soul, can be tapped into. It is not a gift—it is something that anybody can learn to do with training. In fact, I give seminars on how to do just that."

To say the very least, I was floored. My head was swimming, and when we said goodbye, I was exhausted and insanely invigorated at the same time. Who on earth could I possibly tell such a story?

Of course, I told Tilghman the minute she got home from school. She was chagrined to hear the part about Buzz feeling discarded and headed to the barn post haste. I also called Lynda, who had referred me to the psychic, to tell her too. It was madness. It was bizarre. It was *thrilling!* Naturally I had to drive to Teri's new barn to tell her that Buzz missed her animals, and slowly but surely, I began to *believe* that Jeri had truly communicated with Buzz. It didn't take me long to reach that conclusion, and I am steadfast in that belief.

Bill and my son, Will, were intrigued, to say the least, but Bill would join right in with the naysayers when they scoffed and laughed at my ridiculous naiveté. Surely this woman had some computer that helped her conjure up these "revelations." How sad that I, an intelligent woman, could be so deluded. But the skeptics could not explain how Jeri came up with the cat and dog story or how she knew about the swimming and foxhunting. I never revealed to Jeri the name of our barn, so how would she have found out the size of my saddle or that Buzz wore a red blanket?

There was just too much undeniable and verifiable truth to process here, and I suppose I *wanted* to believe her. How wonderful—a possible introduction to a new dimension and removal of the blinders issued at birth!

When I told Jeri that I had intuited his injury—albeit in a somewhat different scenario—she told me that I already knew because Buzz had told me. "Animals are always telling us things if we can learn to listen," she said. Whoa...I suppose I believe this on a very *basic* level because one can read dogs' and horses' general conditions pretty easily by their eyes and body language. But to interpret my intuition of Buzz's mishap as communication from him was astonishing.

The fact that some people are simply more attuned than others to animals has always intrigued me. What vibes do they get that I don't? I suppose I *was* acting on my gut instinct by seeking whatever unconventional help I could find for Buzz, but I was sure missing his cues (all those attempted bites) along the way. Fascinating.

Chapter 19

Someone, during the many narrations of this story, gave me the name of another horse psychic whom they had used, and I *had* to call her as well. One should always seek a second opinion in any medical situation, right? It was important to me to see if any of Jeri's insights could be corroborated—whatever *that* means in this hazy, nebulous new dimension. And the experience was no less amazing and satisfying.

This second communicator also couldn't get over how funny Buzz was. In fact, he was, without a doubt, the funniest horse she had ever talked to! Any and all who came in contact with Buzz said the same thing. Buzz told her that he really liked black leg wraps (we used navy blue for daily riding) and that he thought running martingales were pretty cool. A running martingale is a leather aid that keeps a horse from throwing his head too high with small rings that "run" along the reins. Ours was a less expensive standing model that attached to the bridle noseband. He also said that we had made him a better horse and that he had learned lots of new stuff!

The injury details were confirmed with this second call, so I knew what needed to be done. I ran right out and bought a new pair of *black* leg wraps (the running martingale was too expensive) and called my friend Mary Lu McFadyen to see if she had room in her four-stall barn in Redmond for a big grey goofball. At her place, Buzz would be free to go in and out of his stall and run around with other horses in a large three-acre pasture, even in the moonlight if he wished. More importantly, he would be able to heal his tender back. I was elated when she said yes.

Mary Lu came to pick him up in her two-horse trailer, and Buzz whinnied so loudly the whole way to his new home that Tilghman and I could hear him in our car following behind. I said to Tilghman that he must be bidding a sad farewell to his pals at Evergreen, but she said, and I believe more correctly, that he was shouting for joy! He was going to a great new home and was thrilled to be doing so. Hooray, hooray, hooray. And, for heaven's sake, don't even think that he couldn't know. We had told him!

Part V

Lacrimae Rerum

If a poet knows more about a horse than he does about heaven, he might better stick to the horse, and some day the horse may carry him to heaven.

Charles Ives, composer

Chapter 20

Life at Mary Lu's was good. Buzz had two pasture mates to run and play with—more accurately run and *bite* with. My word, his hide had more holes than Swiss cheese. He was doing, though, what horses are supposed to do—run free and constantly graze. With his head always reaching for the ground, he was able to stretch his top line and allow his back to recover. What a happy horse he was. Never *ever* again did Buzz try to bite me, and our relationship took an entirely new turn.

Before the conversation with the psychics, I always felt that I was the alpha partner—it was my position to make him do my bidding. After all, he was a horse and it was my responsibility to train him, using a touch of whip and a heavy hand to convince him, if necessary. I had been brought up watching people deal with recalcitrant horses in various ways, and that mostly meant using a switch and a loud, menacing voice. Unfortunately, this is still, for the most part, the prevailing practice. The "horse whisperer" concept of training (made famous by Monte Roberts and Buck Brannaman), whereby one reads a horse's body language and mimics the alpha mare in a herd, was not in the picture in my formative years. The new horsemanship training was only just beginning to take flight during my time together with Buzz.

When Buzz tried to bite me, it always resulted in my whacking him soundly with my riding crop and giving a solid jerk on the reins for good measure. And, actually, I'm pretty sure that if I *had* known the new horsemanship methods, I probably would have done exactly the same thing. I, however, am ashamed to relate how badly I lost my temper one day when Buzz threw his head down, jerking me forward out of the saddle, and thus snapping my neck and back rather hard. The behavior on his part was bad, but Teri called me down when I whipped him more than twice.

The punishment should be once to get his attention and a second time for the misbehavior—or some such ridiculous reasoning—but I was really mad, and it truly hurt when he snapped my spine in half, so I hit him once to get his attention, a second time for the misbehavior, a third time for my pain, a fourth time for making me mad, and I probably whacked him a fifth time just because. Of course, in my fury, I didn't hesitate to remind Teri that she had beat the living daylights out of a huge horse named Pee Wee when riding with me on the trails one day (Pee Wee deserved it though—even if he was a good jumper—he had tried to kill a lot of us during his career). But not once did I consider what had caused Buzz to do the dirty deed to begin with.

Most bad behavior in horses can be attributed to pilot error. There are some horses, unquestionably, that are just plain mean, but I suspect that unless there is some problem or defect at birth they were not wired that way. Others might dispute that point. I suppose the debate of nature versus nurture could arguably apply to the personalities of horses because, indeed, some horses *are* sweet and docile, and others are nasty and difficult. But I strongly believe that our treatment of these magnificent animals has bearing on their behavior, and when treated well, most horses do everything in their power to please.

Horses are powerful creatures that *must* be willing to please if they let us ride them, and then they allow us to train them to perform all manner of tricks for

125

our enjoyment. I have often heard people say how much their horse loves to jump or perform intricate dressage maneuvers, and I often agreed that Buzz was in that camp. Being compliant in all our endeavors, he seemed to truly enjoy himself. Buzz was a good jumper, and dressage was beginning to be a winning pursuit, but I have to smile when facing the truth. What horse have you ever seen, when left to his own devices—free in a pasture or arena—leap over jumps just for the fun of it or perform a passage or canter pirouette for practice on his own? For the most part, it just doesn't normally happen.

My point is that horses are immensely lovely animals that do incredible things with a willing heart, if asked in a fair and caring manner. A talented Grand Prix rider once said that riding a horse to a five-foot jump was a 60/40 proposition—60 percent of the result was whether the horse wanted to do it, and 40 percent was the expertise of the rider. I'm not so sure that the ratio isn't more like 70/30 or 80/20. Twelve hundred pounds or more of horse is a pretty big thing to boss around if there isn't some measure of harmony and understanding. It is exactly this principle that, to me, makes riding an endeavor unlike any other. What other sport requires working with another living being that outweighs you by a thousand pounds or more? And without complicity how does one succeed at riding?

All of this brings me back to my relationship with Buzz after our talk with the psychics. My mindset was forever changed, and I listened to Buzz like I never had before. We had a patent new understanding, and we had marvelous fun. Our time before all of this was incredible as I never got off his back without saying aloud, for any and all to hear, "I *adore* this horse." But the time spent after this watershed experience was even better. If only it could have lasted longer.

Chapter 21

Buzz continued to flourish at Mary Lu's. His back got better, and we had a whole new world of riding possibilities open up to us. There were trails upon trails to discover and a hunter barn nearby when we were itching for some proper lessons. Getting to these trails usually required a fair amount of street travel, and Buzz was always a trooper in traffic. Trail rides after moving to Mary Lu's were completely different than our trail rides in Bridle Trails Park.

At Bridle Trails, I had to use a strong rubber Pelham bit on Buzz to keep control when we galloped about, but after living freely in an open pasture, Buzz was not as "buzzed." He didn't seem as wild or strong. Two or three trail rides made me take notice of his new behavior. The improved conduct, coupled with an obvious resistance to take the stronger bit—was I listening?—convinced me that he no longer needed the extra power play. I switched to the softer snaffle bit that

I normally used in my lessons, and it was a smart move. He *happily* accepted that bit and rewarded me with delightful manners.

Being less buzzed, though, didn't mean being less fun, as there were plenty of new, never-before-experienced, scary phenomena to keep us on our toes. One such horrifying phenomenon that we encountered on the trails, whether alone or with Mary Lu, was a colossal grey bolder that, to Buzz, must have seemed to vibrate as we rode by. No matter how many times we passed that rock, Buzz jumped four or five feet sideways to avoid being eaten by it. Because Buzz refused to follow any horse, Mary Lu was always behind me, and she never failed to laugh her tail off at my attempts to keep mine in the saddle. I could never understand how seeing someone so near catastrophe was quite so funny, but apparently it was.

The giant stone never failed to spook Buzz, and even though I was prepared forever after, I never failed to amuse Mary Lu. What made *me* laugh was the huge snort Buzz made every time we passed. What in the world did he see that I couldn't? He was probably just messing with me.

This newfound partnership and gloriously relaxed living environment was unfortunately short lived. Bill and I were in St. Thomas, Virgin Islands, on a business trip when tragedy struck. I returned to our hotel room one afternoon to see a message waiting on our phone. The voice was one I did not know. It was a vet from Pilchuck Veterinary Hospital in Snohomish telling me that Buzz had had an accident and was being treated at the clinic. I confess this news was no less alarming than if one of my children had been taken to the ER at Harborview Hospital in Seattle, the top trauma center in the area.

A call to her brought crushing news that Buzz had found barbed wire in his pasture and had badly cut his pastern (the area between the heel of his hoof and the fetlock joint), severing the artery, tendons and tendon sheath. Miraculously, he had not bled to death. It felt like someone had punched me in the stomach—I was finding it hard to breathe. She had operated on him that morning, and his prognosis was not very good—few horses are ever sound after this injury. She *carefully* told me that most horses are euthanized unless they are valuable broodmares. Obviously, the words were not registering well because I asked her if he would ever jump again. She said he would not, and then I asked if we would at least be able to trail ride. She hesitated, saying with measured words that he probably would not recover. But if he was very lucky, depending on his healing, there might be a slim chance of quiet trail riding. I was *devastated.*

I called Mary Lu to see what had happened, and she related the whole story of her day. Hurrying to get to a meeting on time, she noticed Buzz standing in the pasture, not too far from the barn, with head hung especially low. This was not normal, so she went quickly to investigate—she was running late. Blood, mud and an angry wound greeted her, and her plans were immediately altered.

A call to Tom Hansen, our vet, at 8:30 a.m. and a second one to Alison Ashbaugh, a friend with a large horse van, who knew the way to Pilchuck Hospital, got speedy results. Tom came as soon as possible to clean the wound, administer antibiotics and block a nerve so that Buzz could be on his way, and Alison arrived very soon thereafter to swiftly rush him to the hospital. Because of Mary Lu's quick action in getting the help that was needed, did Buzz possibly have a fighting chance?

A thorough investigation of the property commenced as there were two other horses living there. The crippling barbed wire, rusty and tangled, was found down in the front part of the pasture—plenty of blood to lead the way. It had been completely hidden by blackberry brambles and overgrown woody bushes. Its existence was a complete surprise.

Buzz, my Curious George, had found it, though, and my heart aches to think of what he must have gone through when caught in its grip.

The fact that the severed artery spasmed and didn't cause him to bleed to death was very peculiar, but I was thankful for small miracles. I cried in fits and starts all the way home from St. Thomas, trying not to think about how awful it was going to be to put this beautiful animal down. He was only twelve years old, an age in Thoroughbreds at which they are "just getting good," and we were both just getting good with our new-found alliance. *Lacrimae rerum*—the sadness and tears of things.

Chapter 22

Our return was met with more bad news. Tilghman was almost hysterical that Tar Heel, our Springer Spaniel, was bleeding into his water bowl. She reported that he couldn't lap the water up without regurgitating it and some blood back into the bowl. And she was right—his water was pink. His mouth wouldn't close completely—it was agape just a bit—and no amounts of prodding and peering down his throat could reveal the source of the blood. In my fragile state, I asked Bill to please take care of Tar Heel because I needed to get to Pilchuck to see Buzz.

Bill took Tar Heel to the vet and was quickly referred to a specialist who pronounced him to be afflicted with "dropsy," a neurological impairment that might or might not resolve itself. When Bill asked about the bleeding, the vet said it would take a probe to locate the source and quoted a price that Bill was not willing to pay just yet. He brought the dog home, and I decided to call Jeri, the psychic, to see what she could tell us.

Tar Heel lay quietly in the laundry room while I sat at the kitchen table to make my call. I watched him intently while she was communicating with him, but nothing remarkable happened. Jeri reported that Tar Heel had run and skidded across our black and white tile kitchen floor (I can assure you that I did not tell her we had a black and white tile floor), crashing into the doorjamb and knocking his jaw out of alignment. The blood was a result of his scraping the side of his mouth when he tried to chew his food. I instantly turned his lip up and saw three striations that were red and raw, but were not bleeding at the moment. Bingo!

For the next three days, I massaged his jaw, telling him he had a bit of TMJ disorder, and his mouth soon went right back into alignment. Bill was beginning to see why I believed in Jeri's communication skills. She not only helped us fix our pup, but she also saved Bill a wad of dough!

I met Mary Lu the morning after our arrival home to drive to Pilchuck Animal Hospital. My stomach was doing acrobatics as we drove. I was numb and trying hard to hold it together because I knew this was going to be terribly difficult. We walked into the clinic and were directed to a large antiseptic room that had all manner of equipment and operating areas along its perimeter with an empty working space, where we stood, in the center. A door, the size of any door in your house (I relate this because it, surprisingly, was so small), opened at the far end, and in waltzed my handsome beast. Led by an aide, Buzz was in his red quilted blanket with a huge silver moon-boot-looking contraption on his left leg. He *was not* limping at all, though, and when I called his name, he pricked his ears, turned toward me and came looking for carrots. I lost control. I just plain lost it. How on earth was I going to have the guts to put this gorgeous horse down?

I cried, he nuzzled and I held tight to his big strong neck. The vet came in and proceeded to tell me that Buzz was an amazing, strong individual and that if any horse had a chance at healing from this injury, Buzz would be the one. There I stood trying to steel myself for his certain demise—I could hardly believe my ears. She went on to say he was just too strong a character to give up on quite yet and that after a few more days, we could take him home and try nursing him back to health.

She joined the legion of Buzz admirers when she told me what a funny horse I had.

The vet sent us home with a box full of a vast number of syringes, needles and medicines. I was thankful that Mary Lu was with me to double check the directions. We were to give him three medications (gentocin, penicillin, and butazolidin) in the catheter that was embedded in his neck vein, with a saline flush between each med. Each step required a new needle and syringe.

With immense appreciation that the catheter was in place, I recalled the few times that I had tried, on my own, to administer meds with a syringe. They had been less than satisfactory. I just didn't quite have the moxie to drive a needle into his neck with conviction, much less know how to find a vein. One of the meds, we were cautioned, had to be given very slowly. The aide at Pilchuck had administered it too quickly, and Buzz had fallen like a house. Good Lord, this was not the kind of thing I needed to hear.

The meds were to be administered every six hours for a minimum of two weeks. That meant 6:00 a.m., 12:00 noon, 6:00 p.m. and midnight. Mary Lu, being the incredible friend that she was, offered to do

138

the 6:00 a.m. and midnight shifts since he lived in her front yard. I was so grateful for her help because it would have been extremely difficult for me to handle that alone.

Chapter 23

The day arrived to bring Buzz home, and Alison once again did the honors. When the truck pulled up to the barn, she walked into the back to retrieve him. She told us to *stand back* because she had a rocket ship on her hands. Here came Buzz, about as worked up as I've ever seen a horse, lathered with sweat and the whites of his eyes blazing. He came charging off the ramp of the truck with Alison hanging on for dear life. He practically dragged her down the aisle of the small barn, bolted into his stall and proceeded to run frantically around that small cubicle like the tigers in *Little Black Sambo* who ran and ran around the tree until they turned into butter. Buzz didn't look too lame to me!

My gosh, my heart and hopes were soaring sky high, but I was terrified that his maniacal twirling was going to further injure his foot. Having no idea what put him in that state, I knew calming him quickly was of utmost importance, or else. Sitting quietly in the manger I cooed and whoaed, and little by little he calmed down.

It was February—quite chilly outside—and there was the possibility he'd colic or catch cold, so every towel available was used to dry him off. It was a long time before he was dry enough to wear his blanket, and by then it was time to medicate him. My hands were shaking like a leaf the first go, but all went smoothly. I sang "You Are My Sunshine, My Only Sunshine" all the way through while giving the drug we had been cautioned about. No way was he going to crash on me, and from then on, tears rose each and every time I got to the part where I sang, "Please don't taake my Sunshine awaaay."

Our next two weeks were going to be crucial, to say the least, and the fact that he was going to be confined to his stall had me concerned. Thoroughbreds and confinement are not good bedfellows, and there was nothing I could do about it. A windstorm two nights later had Buzz standing three legged the next morning, so something *had* to be done.

I called Jeri. Big surprise! I told her that Buzz had a grave injury that necessitated his being very calm. He had to be good or this injury would not heal and we would ultimately lose him. Whatever Jeri said to him must have hit its mark because Buzz was completely at ease from that moment forward. No more startled responses to every leaf that blew by his window, no more snorting and weaving about the stall and no more pulling and tugging on the lead line when I walked down the aisle *once* per day. He was, indeed, sterling.

In addition to the daily meds, Buzz had to have his bandage changed daily. This required Tom the vet because it was a *process*. The "moon boot" was nothing but strips of duct tape fashioned into a large square that fit over mountains of gauze and a baby diaper to keep out moisture and dirt. The aide at Pilchuck showed us how to make the boot by placing about five or six strips of tape, each about two feet long, on a door and crisscrossing additional strips until there was a solid square mass of tape. This square, placed on the bottom of his hoof, was brought up to cover the gauze and diaper—similar to wrapping a bottle— and additional tape was wrapped around his leg to hold everything in place. It was brilliantly simple and quite slick.

The first time Tom exposed the wound, though, I was stunned. I had never seen such a large gaping space of raw tissue in my life. Buzz's entire pastern from stem to stern had been debrided and scraped clean, and the opportunity for infection was enormous. Nothing was to touch that wound except for a saline wash, so keeping the working area clean and draft free was of utmost importance. Buzz was initially tranquilized for these bandage changes because of his normal behavior in the crossties, but he was extremely good as time went on (thank you Jeri) and the "tranquing" was no longer necessary.

This was our daily routine for two weeks. Each day I would walk Buzz up and down the aisle, and Tom would evaluate his gait. Each day was better than the last, and I was beginning to think that hope was not lost, that Buzz might beat the odds.

Chapter 24

Tom had to be out of town for several days, leaving the bandage-changing to Mary Lu and me, but we were confident by this time that we could do it, and high fives were in order after our first attempt. But after a few days Buzz began to limp a little when I walked him down the aisle. Upon Tom's return, his face all too clearly revealed his reaction to Buzz's limp. He upped the dosage of bute, and the next day there was improvement.

We were a little over two weeks into this regimen by now, and healing was either going to continue to go well or adhesions were going to form. The following day, though, Tom described his lameness as moderate, and my gut was telling me to steel myself. I implored Tom to be as straightforward with me as possible, and if Buzz's lameness reached a point where he felt there was no hope of reversal, to put it to me firmly and not let my emotional attachment to Buzz get in the way.

That day arrived far too soon. Monday, March 8, 1999, the *very next morning*, Buzz came out of his stall three legged. He could barely hobble out to be examined. Tom looked at me, and my heart stopped. There was no denying what needed to happen. Adhesions were forming around the suspensory and flexor tendons, and his fetlock was becoming enlarged. He called the vet at Pilchuck to inquire about a second surgery, but she advised against it, saying the results would certainly be no better. This foot was not going to support him, and other problems would surely arise as a result.

Consider what happened to the racehorse, Barbaro, when he fractured his hind leg in the Preakness. His other feet fell apart like a house of cards. I couldn't bear to watch this happen to Buzz. I remember my father asking if we could amputate his leg—thinking that dogs are quite capable of living three legged—but I explained that horses have very fragile feet and legs and are unable to support their considerable weight on less than all four. A condition known as laminitis develops, wherein the hoof wall separates from the bone. There are many causes of laminitis and

146

lameness is one of them. The pain that would eventually result would be dreadful.

With choking emotion and tears in my eyes, I asked Tom to please put him down right away, but he had to tend to other matters first. He would have to come later in the day. My heart was breaking in two. The reality of what was going to happen hit me with such force that, for a second time, I could barely breathe. And now I would have to *wait*. The first thing I did was turn Buzz out into the pasture with his pals because at this point it certainly didn't matter that he might harm his foot. But his apparent pain kept him subdued. I knew right then that I was making the right choice, even if that choice would fill me with a crippling guilt. Playing God is never easy.

I went home and called Tilghman and Bill, leaving messages to tell them what time Tom would be returning. I stocked up on apples and sugar cubes, and because it was raining and gloomy, I could only keep singing, with wavering voice, "Rainy days and Mondays al-l-l-ways get me down." I returned to the barn to organize all of Buzz's gear, clean his stall and simply gaze at him in the pasture. The wait was horrible. Tilghman arrived before Tom, thank goodness, and we spent quite a while feeding Buzz his treats. Tom finally arrived around 4:30 or 5:00 o'clock. Bill was not there, but I hoped he had gotten my message.

My anxiety grew regarding how Buzz would fall. Anyone who has witnessed horse euthanasia will attest that the reaction is almost instant and that the horse falls stiff-legged like a tree. To make matters worse, Buzz was skittish around Tom. After all the tranquilizer shots he had received over the years for various reasons, and especially of late, Buzz could become agitated just upon hearing Tom's voice. There was nothing I could do about that, but I hated the thought of his being nervous and uneasy during his last moments.

A suitable spot that was open and easily accessible had to be chosen because taking care of a horse's remains (if not buried on the premises) is the job of rendering plants, and I can assure you that his being loaded onto a truck and hauled away was one part of this scenario I was *not* going to witness. A nice grassy spot near the driveway was chosen. Tilghman and I removed Buzz's blanket and brought him over to Tom. I was cautioned to leave the lead rope quite long to avoid getting a burn, and with Buzz's eye trained on Tom, the sodium pentobarbital was injected intravenously.

I do not know if Tom gave him a sedative with the barbiturate, but Buzz's fall to earth was his final gift to me. Instead of falling hard, Buzz's hind legs slowly buckled, and he rolled to his side, just like he would do if he were going to roll in the grass.

Tilghman and I fell to our knees, weeping, and I kept stroking his head, repeating over and over "I'm so sorry, Buzzy, I'm so sorry." His tongue was hanging out, and I kept trying to push it back in because I couldn't bear to see the ugly reality of sudden death. Tom was right by our side, administering more of the drug in case the dosage was not enough. He had tears in his eyes, and I remember thinking how hard this must be for him to do over and over again.

Buzz took three rattling gasps of air, and then Tom touched Buzz's eye to check for a corneal reflex. When Buzz did not blink, Tom pronounced him dead. I knew immediately the moment it happened because the change in Buzz's eye was absolute. That eye, with those curious little globular balls in the pupil that can be seen when sunlight shines brightly inside, went from glossy dark brown to a dull blue-grey. It was like a shade being drawn—one moment Buzz was there, and the next instant he was gone. He had drawn his tongue in too,

149

and my big beautiful grey horse that I loved more than I can ever begin to describe was still.

Chapter 25

Bill arrived right after Tom had left and when he saw the huge tarp that was draped over Buzz, he burst into tears. We knelt down to pat him, and Bill recalled his fondest of memories; breathing in and out nostril to nostril (the best way to introduce yourself to a horse) and feeding a vodka tonic from his hand; watching Buzz rear and buck and race around the arena when turned out of his stall and then calmly walking over for a pat. We laughed about the time I had brought our son, Will, and a friend to the barn to pick up Tilghman. Buzz had put that big head of his through the sunroof of my car, scaring the bejeesus out of both boys and truly looking like the T. rex from Jurassic Park.

Kneeling there with Buzz was a sad, sad moment with us laughing and crying at the same time, but I'll love Bill forever for being so dear.

The next few days were miserable. I was at a loss as to what to do with myself. There were no more meds to administer or bandages to change, and the hole in my heart was enormous. Word spread like wildfire, and the cards and calls started pouring in. There is no understanding of the depth of grief for such a loss like the understanding of a fellow horseman. Virtual strangers sent me cards saying that after years they still mourn their best friend.

What is it about a *horse* that makes losing it so painful? Nine dogs have graced and enriched my life from the time I was a little girl. Some of them had to be put down while others either ran away or died of natural causes. I grieved for every one of those dogs—I adored them—but nothing compares to the sadness I experienced with Buzz. His spirit and utter charm were enormous—perhaps even commensurate with his stature—but the size of the animal, surely, is not the gauge by which one measures affection toward it. Of course not. Our connection, I believe, was simply one of those "once in a lifetime" special happenings.

A dear friend's mother helped shape a belief many years ago that I still embrace today. She said everyone possesses an energy that touches, in varying degrees, each person met during a lifetime. Some people have more energy or spirit than others. It is the strength of that spirit, she believed, that lives on in our memory of that person. I now believe every living thing possesses that energy, and more than just sustaining a memory, I believe that the energy remains constant. It doesn't change. It may move from one realm to another, but it does not change. After talking to Jeri and reading more about the science of energy, I am more convinced that the idea of a soul or spirit does not only apply to humans but to all living things. Buzz's enormous energy and spirit were felt by all who came in contact with him. And I *saw*, in his eyes, Buzz's spirit leave him that day.

Nothing is more sacred as the bond between a horse and rider...no other creature can ever become so emotionally close to a human as a horse.

When a horse dies, the memory lives on because an enormous part of his owner's heart, soul, very existence dies also... but that can never be laid to rest, it is not meant to be.

Stephanie M Thorn

Chapter 26

Very soon after Buzz's death, I had a funny dream that still makes me laugh. I always said that if I ever bought another horse, it needed to be a black-and-white Paint with one buttock black and the other one white. My show name for this horse would be Demi Derriere and his nickname Half Ass. In my dream, I received a call from someone to come and see a brand-new black-and-white Paint colt. He was just beautiful. While I stroked his head, I gazed into his eyes and felt a tremendous presence of Buzz. I whispered, "Buzz, is that *you*?" and the colt reached out and bit my boob! I awoke howling with laughter. That Big Blue Boob-Biting Buzzard was never going to die.

This experience with Buzz changed so many things for me. The crazy, kooky palm readers, energy-healers and various esoterics are not so crazy and kooky anymore. Maybe, just maybe, these people know something that most of us don't want to know or are afraid to know. Believing that Jeri communicated with

Buzz and Tar Heel has led me to have a much broader understanding of where I fit in this universe—*of what consequence my thinking and believing have in shaping my life.*

My spiritual beliefs have morphed considerably. I feel differently about organized religion. The nagging questions that have plagued me, long before Buzz, about which religion is the chosen one—which dogmas to believe and which ones to only give lip service—don't bother me as much anymore. Perhaps part of my changing philosophies is a result of getting older, but my experience with Buzz has surely been a catalyst in my digging ever deeper.

I now believe that plants and trees are sentient on a basic and fundamental level. Call *me* a kook, but the books on that subject are fascinating. Each day that I spend in my garden, I talk to my plants, and I think of Buzz every time. A few years ago, Will's fraternity brother spent several days with Bill and me while he was traveling on the West Coast. It was April, and the perennials in my garden were just starting to emerge. I praised their beauty vociferously and thanked them for returning each time I passed by. When this young man returned to Chapel Hill, he said to Will, "I had a great time with your parents, but, Dude, your mother *talks* to her plants!"

These new ways of thinking are exhilarating and fascinating, and the horizon is beyond reach. I have found a new lifelong endeavor, full of more surprises than I ever imagined. Everyday I have some reason to thank Buzz for the course I am on.

Buzz and Tilghman at Mary Lu McFadyen's
barn...his last and happiest home.

Buzz at Bridle Trails State Park meeting Twinkle,
Caitlyn Cushman's pony, who "bobbed and weaved"
in his stall. Buzz loved to schmooze.

"Umm…you smell good!"

Nothing was safe around Buzz.

Gimme that hat.

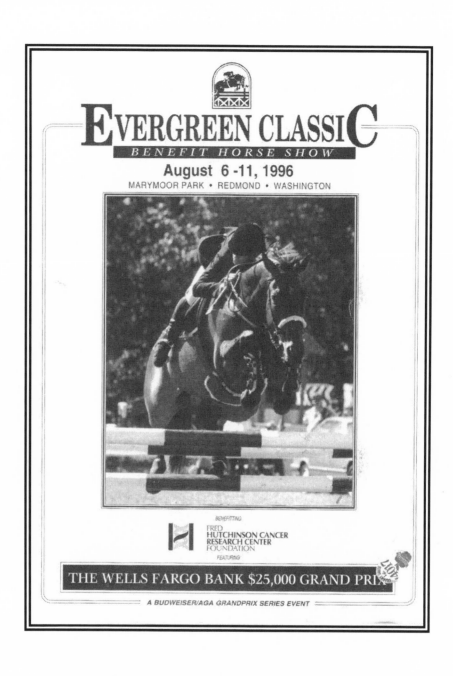

The Evergreen Classic horseshow program.

161

Part VI

Epilogue

You took care of your horse, and your horse took care of you.

Elton Gallegly politician

The love of horses knows not its own depth till the hour of separation.

Unknown

Chapter 27

One year after Buzz died, I sat at my kitchen table, reflecting on how much I still missed him on this sad anniversary. While thumbing through a magazine, one of those pesky 4 x 5 inserts fell on the floor. I reached down to pick it up and to this day have no *idea* what was being advertised and am furthermore astonished that I failed to save the card, but on a vivid hot-pink background were four letters, in green, orange, blue and red. Those letters, cheery, colorful and bright were…B U Z Z.

My eyes filled and then overflowed with tears. I cried hard. But as I wept, I gradually began to wonder if I possibly found this card for a reason. Was it a message? My mind was fielding all manner of questions—does that sort of thing really occur? Finally, and I realize this may sound a bit delusional, but after everything that had happened, I chose to believe that it was so. My tears slowly ebbed with eventual gratitude because deep inside my soul, I imagined Buzz was telling me that all was well. The following quotations, authors unknown, say so much. They speak to what every horse lover knows implicitly.

The love for a horse is just as complicated as the love for another human being…if you never love a horse, you will never understand.

A person that has a dog or cat has a companion. A person that has a horse has a treasure in their heart, a sparkle in their eyes and more love than the whole world

Riding is for those people who see not a horse but a spirit next to them.

The following is a verse I wrote two days after Buzz died. It, along with several pictures and tack, hangs in my office. A fly whisp, which a wonderful saddler fashioned out of Buzz's tail and my riding crop, hangs there as well. His shoes are serving duty in my kitchen as a good luck talisman and doorstop.

GOODBYE

My lovely friend
My handsome beast
My funny clown
I miss you.
My purest pleasure
My simple joy
My silly fool
I miss you.
You read my mind
You fed my soul
You made me laugh
I miss you.
You taught me trust
You showed me love
You made me proud
I miss you.
Be good my friend
Walk true my steed
And watch over me
If you can.
I love you Buzzy.
Goodbye.

167

Afterword

With the true appreciation of life comes the responsibility of ensuring a humane death.

Diana Berry

No heaven can heaven be, if a horse isn't there to welcome me.

Unknown

~

In relating the incredible love and support that I received upon Buzz's death I left out an important part—due partly because of wanting to "stay on task" and not derail my emphasis on Buzz, but also because the impact at the time was a little overpowering. Including it here in the afterword feels right, as something that needs to be done in respect for a special person.

Diana Berry, a wonderful friend as well as riding companion, was a compatriot in grief at the same time I was dealing with Buzz's mortal injury. Her wonderful horse, Barney, had been put down *one week* before Buzz because of a broken leg he had sustained while goofing off in his pasture. I had encouraged Diana to move Barney to a barn in Redmond, just as I had done, because of the open pasture and the happiness he'd experience. I was feeling terribly guilty for that persuasive advice.

Barney was not just Diana's horse; he was very special to me as well. I leased him for almost two years while Diana underwent bone-marrow transplant and endless chemotherapy for ovarian cancer, and it was an honor to be able to help Diana during her ordeal. Because of his exuberance and beauty, Barney grabbed my heart almost instantly. A handsome muscular chestnut with a white blaze and boundless energy, this horse was Diana's dearest charge. He was a terrific jumper and a wonderfully entertaining trail horse.

A long list of do's and don'ts from Diana cataloguing what to expect from him during my lease included the following warning, "If you come upon a freshly cut log or tree, he may be very reticent to move past it. My feeling is that he has a problem with the light-colored part. I often dismount and lead him past the obstacle." That just cracked me up. Really. The light-colored part was what scared him? Incredibly, Barney *did* snort and halt in front of any newly fallen tree, and I always asked him if it was the light-colored part that offended him, but I never had to dismount him to get past it. We had a pretty tacit understanding regarding such an action…it wasn't going to happen.

Barney's show name was Lionheart—a classy and apt name for his physique and courage over jumps, but no so fitting in the park when approaching fresh cut timber! It always tickled me that his informal barn name was *Barney*, but it fitted him well. He and I grew to have a terrific bond, and in reality it was quite hard to hand over my stewardship of him when Diana got better and was able to resume his care. He and I realized tremendous success in many horseshows and advanced clinics, and I just plain loved him. Interestingly, Buzz arrived on the scene almost immediately after I had to relinquish Barney back to Diana. Many people commented that it was difficult to get used to my presence on a grey horse after seeing me for two years on a handsome chestnut. It took time to become attached to Buzz, but certainly not a long time…his personality won me over in short order.

Diana had a memorial service for Barney to which, curiously, she did not invite me. Her reasoning was she didn't feel it was fair for me to have to come to where Barney had died when I was going through such trauma with Buzz. I am sorry she made that decision because it would have been my heartfelt desire to attend, but she did it out of true concern for me. I want to share an email she sent, describing the gathering, because it was a tremendous help at that time.

Dear Lean,

I wish to tell you about Barney's memorial service. First, I want you to know that I talked about your relationship with Barney, and how much you cared for him, and people talked about how great the two of you were together. I said that you were going through a lot because of Buzz being seriously injured and I hoped I'd made the right decision by not asking you to attend.

There were only six people there who knew Barney and had been involved in his care in some way. Tears were shed by everyone, and stories were shared about Barney, their own feelings when they had lost horses they loved, and even some talk about their awareness of my illness and what a big part Barney had played in keeping me going through it all. So it worked out that three levels of grieving happened— first for Barney, then for the other wonderful horses who had been lost, then for me—all woven together.

I started things off by saying that the Buddha said, "Fortune changes as the swish of a horse's tail." And a little Zen story of a man who was galloping his horse down the road. Someone standing along the roadside yelled out, "Where are you going?" The rider yelled back, "I don't know! Ask the horse!" (The story is supposed to represent disorientation.) Then I talked about how suddenly everything had happened and that I had thought I had everything planned out for Barney; how his future would be taken care of after I died and how he would be happy and secure—but that I hadn't asked HIM. Then people just began to spontaneously chime in offering support. It was very informal, spontaneous and emotional. I addressed each person and shared a memory of something they had done for or with Barney, and my gratitude for their involvement. And what better time to tell you, I have never felt I have expressed to you how wonderful you were to help both me and Barney when I was in such trouble, by leasing him. I trusted you implicitly with him, and felt so privileged that you were there. I have felt such deep gratitude so many times, even thinking about it up to last month, but I don't think I ever really communicated what everything you did for both of us meant to me. Thank you.

Anne (my vet) offered a prayer that started, "Creator of Barney" that was hugely emotional.

Diana went on for a bit longer in her description, but ended with the following paragraph. Diana was a clinical psychologist.

The psychiatric diagnostic manual says that guilt about things done or not done around the time of a loved one's death is a part of normal mourning, and I personally have not met anyone who has put down any animal, who has not experienced guilt afterward. But maybe as time goes on we will recapture the whole picture in our minds, rather than being so focused on how our boys' lives ended, and then we will remember how we lavished our love on them and we will be able to forgive ourselves.

Love, Diana

Those words were a balm for my raw and aching psyche. Diana was a great help to me, and I hope the reverse was true as well. She was a wonderful friend. Her death five years later deeply saddened all who knew her. Diana often spoke of hoping to be with Barney after she died. I *hope* that they are, indeed, together in some form or another, unknown to us all.

Barney at the Lake Washington Saddle Club C-rated show.

An interesting view…love that swishing
tail…*his* that is!

Such an enjoyable mount.

Barney at Bridle Trails…what a handsome face!

ABOUT THE AUTHOR

McLean (Lean) Goodpasture Carroll is a graduate of Hollins College in Roanoke, Virginia with a B.A. in Music which she utilizes as a piano instructor in her home. She started the story of Big Blue Buzzard about eight years ago and says, "It came out of my head and heart with complete abandon. The process was a complete surprise."

Lean lives with her husband, Bill, and their Springer Spaniel, Zach, in Bellevue, Washington and they have two grown children—a son, Will, and a daughter, Tilghman.